The New Lenox Writers' Group Presents:

Animals

All

Around

Compiled by: James Pressler

Previous titles by the New Lenox Writers' Group:

Writers, We

The Place We Call Home

Troubling Times

Memory Lane

A Matter of Faith

A Story For Every Season

All books are available online

Cover design by James Pressler

Cover artwork by

Printed in Century 12 pt.

DEDICATION

Ed "Bull" Treffry

This book is dedicated to the wonderful memory of Ed "Bull" Treffry, the wisdom and mentor of the New Lenox Writer's Group. He was always there for a piece of knowledge or encouraging advice from his beautiful mind, whether about improving your skills as a writer, learning how to tap into the potential inside one's mind or just life in general.

Ed lived a long and full life, telling many stories about his adventures that always encouraged others to believe anything is possible if we just believe in ourselves. He was able to transfer a lot of his stories of life to many self-published children's books that entertained all ages.

His gentle eyes and loving smile will truly be missed as we continue down our path called life. I know he's looking down, patiently waiting for our books to become big-time movies! We love you Ed. Thanks for all of the beautiful memories!

TITLES & AUTHORS

Contents

ix

ACKNOWLEDGMENTS

Special thanks to Jens Schommer, who volunteered his time and talents to photograph the writers and put a face to their names. Furthermore, we are always grateful for the hospitality of the New Lenox Public Library in providing our group a place to hone our craft, and hopefully produce works worthy of gracing your shelves.

Mooned

by Norm Cowie

This is a work of fiction. (That means it's not based on real stuff)

"Sit, roll over, beg."

– Things you probably shouldn't say to a werewolf.

Montrail Melees are trail shoes, a bit expensive perhaps, but excellent for running dirt paths. A pair of these particular shoes slapped onto the earthen ground with controlled precision as Ben Hurdt ran the wooded trail under silvery moonlight. As he approached a small rise between clumps of river birches, he attacked the incline and cleared its summit with ease. He rode gravity down the other side of the meandering path, lengthening his stride to eat yards up at a time.

These midnight runs down a well known path in the forest next to his property were the perfect antidote to a high stress work day, and today had been more stressful than ever.

Herdt took a deep breath of clean air perfumed with the heady aroma of wood, loam, fern, wildlife and... something else.

He was trying to figure out what the something else was

when it landed on him, slamming him to the dirt.

a couple months later

Fetch was lying on the floor, shedding nervously.

Something horrible was happening and the huge shaggy dog didn't have the mental acuity to figure it out. He didn't even know what mental acuity was, which didn't bother him because he had other more useful talents, like the ability to sniff out dropped hotdogs, soak sunlight on his belly and manufacture copious quantities of slobber.

The room was dark, lit mostly by a fire in the fireplace and a silver moonbeam slicing into the room through the window. In the shadows of a bookcase, glittering eyes marked where Cat looked on with feline interest as if having been forewarned of some impending event. The inky black cat's legs were neatly folded under her in a way that belied her ability to erupt into movement.

Fetch ignored the cat, his eyes glued on Alpha, who had been acting and smelling kind of... different... lately. When the smells became the most... interesting... Alpha would lock him in the garage. Fetch never understood, but always forgave Alpha. But Fetch hadn't been locked up tonight.

Tonight, they had been on the couch sharing French fries

and watching TV together. Well, Alpha was watching it. Fetch didn't much appreciate the television, as it smelled hot, plastic and inedible. Not even worth chewing on. As he chomped fries, he hoped Alpha wouldn't finish the whole hamburger. He also kept a wary eye on Cat because, well, she was a competing predator.

Then Alpha stiffened, crying out in pain and anguish.

Fetch surged to his feet, alert and ready to protect. His senses swept the air for whatever had disturbed his pack-mate.

Then Alpha screamed, arching his back in pain. His dinner clattered to the floor.

Normally when food hit the ground, Fetch would gobble it up. Any food that hit the floor was his by pack rules. But pack-ship overrode the instinct for food and Fetch stayed alert, and sniffed at Alpha, trying to figure out what was wrong.

As Fetch inspected his pack-mate, Alpha did something he'd never done before. Ever.

He struck Fetch.

More stunned than hurt, Fetch retreated to the corner of the room behind the rocking chair. He wouldn't abandon Alpha, but instinctively he understood he should back away.

Meanwhile, Alpha threw himself around the room. Tables were knocked over, books spilled from bookcases. He crashed backward against a wall and a tortured sound tore from his throat. Strange shapes rolled under his skin, bones and muscles bunching and pulsating, pushing the skin beyond tolerance. He screamed, screamed again and collapsed to the floor.

Fetch jumped to his feet, nose twitching and ears swiveled forward. He stood, quivering with indecision.

Alpha tried to gain his feet, stumbled and fell over an end table, his skin heaving as if something was trying to escape. Fetch whined, licked his lips nervously and vibrated in confusion.

He slunk forward, whimpering as he got closer to Alpha, who was rocking in agitation. There was a sudden convulsion and Alpha fell backwards, slamming again into the bookcase, and scattering Cat, who leaped onto the sofa with silent agility.

Giving a last painful gasp, Alpha collapsed to the floor.

Fetch took a hesitant step forward, and heard a low voiced growl.

He froze.

There was a moment of tense quiet, and then Alpha rolled to his feet and stood.

Only it wasn't Alpha. It was another canine. Not a dog exactly. A wilder smell, full of pent up fury and something else. As a dog, Fetch could smell emotions, and these were disquieting and disturbing. But through it, his sensitive smell could pick up traces of Alpha.

Where was Alpha?

He crept forward, straining to catch the elusive scent. The other canine stretched, letting the transformation settle bones and muscles, so Fetch came closer. He could almost pick up critical scents. Almost. He ducked his head so he could sniff the other canine's butt. The smells under an animal's tail are like Braille for dogs.

Ah, Alpha. He could smell Alpha.

Body language is important to canines, and if Fetch hadn't been so intent on his mission to read butt language, he wouldn't have missed the other animal's sudden disapproval of his actions.

Suddenly the other canine spun and lashed at Fetch, who yelped as a hot flash of pain erupted in his back leg. Snarling in fear and pain, he tore away and whirled to meet the threat.

They faced each other, heads down, low growls vibrating their chests and lips curving to bare fangs.

The other animal feinted, and struck again, sharp teeth tearing into Fetch's chest. He tried to pull away, but the teeth were like a vice.

Then a yowling snarl split the air and something landed on the other animal's head, needle-like claws clamping on the intruder.

Cat.

The beast reeled and bit at Cat. She hung on with feline strength and tore at the animal's ears. It roared and reached up to rip Cat from his scalp. She spit cat obscenities before being flung against the chair. The monster leaped and huge jaws snapped on the place suddenly vacant of cat.

Spitting out blood and fur... he'd gotten a bit of Cat... the creature snarled and thundered to the open window. With a savage leap, it blasted through the screen into the yard, leaving Fetch frozen in indecision behind it. He was trying to understand what his senses were trying to tell him. He could hear the creature crashing away through the underbrush in the forest. He could still pick up the scent of Alpha, the freshest coming from the path the creature had taken out the window.

Cat was under the table, licking a bleeding tail.

If it was simply a case of following Alpha, Fetch would probably have left right then to follow. But he was still confused by the scent issues.

And he was hungry.

But Alpha. The creature that wasn't Alpha. Should he pursue?

But he was hungry.

He knew he shouldn't go outside without permission. But who was there to give it to him?

And he was hungry.

Then he remembered. There was food on the floor that had

to be dealt with. And he could think better once his belly was full. Then he could figure out what to do about Alpha. Crisis averted, he turned and searched for the hamburger.

Before he could find it, rippling pain shot through his body. Then again. He thumped to the floor, and tried to get back to his feet. Another wave of stabbing hurt rode across his body as if he were encased in an Iron Maiden.

He couldn't understand, and whined for Alpha to come help him.

Alpha didn't come, and Fetch staggered around the room, his head clouded.

If he could have seen himself, he would have seen his body convulsing and muscles contracting and growing and... hurting. It hurt.

He whimpered again.

For a few seconds, or minutes... what's time to a dog... Fetch opened his eyes.

He was lying on his side. The floor felt cold, hard and unfamiliar. With a groan, he tried to roll to his feet. But his body felt awkward and strange, and the roll failed miserably.

"Push up onto your elbow," a voice said, startling him.

He looked around for the source of the voice and vivid impressions exploded into his face. He cried out in a voice he had never heard before.

"It's called 'color," the voice said. "They actually see in more color spectrums than I do." The voice sounded mildly surprised.

As Fetch craned his neck to see who was speaking to him, a spasm of pain tore into his head.

"You're feeling your brain expanding," the voice said helpfully through waves of agony. "It will probably take you longer than it took me."

Fetch dimly registered surprise he could understand, not just the words, the language, but also the concept behind the words, though he still wasn't sure what the unknown speaker was alluding to.

He closed his eyes and put his paws... no, not paws... something else... around his head. His head, another strange thing. It was round. The nose practically non-existent. For that matter, smells were largely non-existent too, but his head was too flooded with pain for this to register.

After a few centuries, years, moments, the pain started receding. His eyes slid open slowly, waiting for another burst of agony. When no pain manifested, he opened his eyes the rest of the way, a riot of color intruding as soon as his eyelids granted it permission.

"Wow!" he breathed.

"Pretty, huh?" the voice said.

"Yeah. What did you call it?"

"Color. Dogs don't see color."

Now Fetch looked up into huge yellow green eyes. The eyes belonged to a human girl perched primly on the counter, legs neatly folded. Her skin was ebony, some impossible exotic blend of African, Indian and the other kind of Indian. Her features were thin and precise, her silky straight black hair shone with the healthy gloss people would spend hundreds to achieve at a salon. She was not wearing... 'clothes,' his mind helpfully supplied the word. That fact held no import to him other than that... 'humans', his mind again supplying a word... generally wore garb to protect their furless bodies.

That was about all Fetch could tell about her. If he could get close enough to sniff her butt, maybe he'd be able to figure other stuff out.

"What happened to me?" he said after a moment.

The girl leaped down with silent grace from the counter. "Here, let me help you up," she said, holding out a hand.

Fetch looked at his paw... no, not paw. There was no paw at

the end of his leg. No, not leg either. 'Arm' his brain helpfully supplied the information. And his brain, where was all of that thought coming from? And memories. Memories were more of a fog before, but now they seemed so clear. And words that never meant anything to him before suddenly meant something. More than just 'here boy,' 'come,' 'sit,' and his favorite, 'good boy.' He had been surrounded by words for years, never understanding, never comprehending. But now, knowledge flooded in.

He held out his arm, and the girl took his hand, pulling him to his feet.

There was a dizzying moment, when his head passed his normal altitude, and then he was standing on his hind legs. No, his only legs. He only had two now.

The girl let go, and he immediately started wobbling back and forth. She grabbed him just before he plummeted to the floor.

He grabbed onto the counter, clutching it like a life raft. His legs felt wobbly and strange, differently jointed.

"Ah, I can't do it."

He dropped to the floor until he was on his hands and feet. He was face down, staring at the vibrantly colored floor. At least it appeared vibrant to his newly enhanced vision. He tried to look up at the girl, but this position hurt his neck. He pulled his very, very long legs under him and heavily fell onto his butt, carefully moving his tail aside as he did so.

Tail?

What tail?

He looked back at his butt.

Where's his tail?!

"You don't have one," the girl said.

From this position he could look at her with relative comfort.

"What?"

"A tail. I don't either. Pity. I love my tail." Then she nonchalantly licked her arm. An expression of distaste crossed her face and she went, "Augh, horrible. And this tongue is way too slick."

Now Fetch knew who the girl was.

"Cat?"

The werewolf thrashed through the woods, hot on the deer's trail. He could see the deer bounding over and through bushes and shrubs, juking right and left, eyes wide with panic.

Whenever possible, the werewolf tried to navigate a direct route, using combined human animal intelligence to outwit the fleet deer. When forced to shift direction, his long bushy tail compensated on the turns.

He was having the time of his life.

Ignoring the branches whipping at his face, the werewolf drew nearer, and a wolfish grin split his face. His tongue lolled, and he felt a rush from the chase. A surge of adrenaline and blood-lust. He imagined ripping into the deer's white belly, the deer's warm life exploding into his mouth like a ripe fruit, his canine fangs ripping and rending into dark, sinewy meat.

His eyes fell shut as he imagined the scene.

Hot blood. The deer's eyes glassy in death. Ripping at meat, tearing it from the bones, which would later yield their own delicious marrow.

Wolves in the wild lack imagination. No one knows why that is. It just is. You won't see a wolf daydreaming or contemplating his future. Perhaps there's a reason for this. Like how important it is that they keep their focus while chasing a deer through the forest in the middle of the night.

Unfortunately, a werewolf retains many of his human qualities.

And it was because of these same human qualities he closed his eyes to daydream. Not for very long. Just for a second. But as a result, he missed the deer's quick burst to the left.

Next thing he knew, he was hurtling through space.

The elongated prehensile nose of an elephant is an incredibly versatile instrument. Sensitive, yet capable of great strength, it can pick up a dime or break a tree trunk with equal ease. The trunk contains no skeletal mass, yet with its many muscles it can virtually move in any direction, curling inward or outward. It's even slightly telescopic, allowing the elephant to reach for objects just slightly out of reach. It can equally be used for communication or as a hose. It's truly one of the most magnificent tools on the planet.

Yet, when a baby elephant is born, the baby has to learn to use its trunk. And until it does, its trunk just flops around uselessly. The baby must rely on its mother to help it eat and learn to use its trunk.

Fetch knew nothing of this, and had it been brought to his attention, he would perhaps share some understanding with the baby elephant. He knew how to work a tail, but the body he was in had no tail. It did have thumbs, though, which was a new concept for Fetch.

Perhaps if all dogs had thumbs, they might have had to adapt to them with greater sized brains. Now Fetch had the brain, and he had the thumbs. But using them was another matter entirely.

Cat was padding softly around the living room, exploring everything from a new perspective.

"What are you doing?" Fetch asked.

She paused, and gave him the intense look cats use under all circumstances except those rare occasions when catnip rattles their brains.

"Exploring," she answered, after a moment where she might have been deciding if she wanted to answer.

"How come I can understand you?" Fetch asked. There was another question that he couldn't quite formulate in his mind. Something about how pleasing ... and something ... Cat looked in her new form. Especially now that they were wearing much the same forms now for the first time ever.

She paused again. It was weird how she retained much of a cat's grace in a new body. "Our brains adapted to our new bodies. Obviously, the transition from beast to human brought with it the abilities and mental abilities of our new physiological shapes."

"Huh?"

"In your case, it was an increase in mental prowess. In mine, a decrease. I feel severely limited in both shape and intellect."

Fetch felt he ought to be offended, but dogs don't offend easily. "What? You couldn't speak before."

Even in this form, her eyes were large and intense. "Couldn't? Perhaps the more operative word is 'wouldn't."

"Huh?"

She finally blinked, and then went back to exploring the place where Alpha broke through the window. She carefully stepped around the broken glass, and then her gaze went to the wooded area in the back yard.

Fetch realized he was hungry.

He hooked an arm on a dining room chair and pulled himself back onto shaky feet. He stood, swaying slightly, his body's internal gyros compensating for the dizzying distance from his face to the ground. Then gravity pushed him from his unsteady alliance with balance, and he started leaning to the left. He tried to compensate the other direction, but once gravity grabbed hold, the joker wouldn't let go. He ran sideways a couple steps before crashing into a counter. He grabbed the top like a drowning man.

Cat tried to cock an ear at him, but when it didn't swivel the way it should have, she turned and watched him stumble around the kitchen, a Mona Lisa smile on her face.

Fetch saw her amusement, and it gave him resolve to conquer this two legged thing. He refused to drop to all four again. Grimly, he pushed away from the counter and tried to dig his toe nails into the floor. But the flat things on top of his toes proved inadequate to the task and he went down again.

Cat was mumbling to herself. "They can't see. They can't smell. They can't hear. How did they ever get to the top of the food chain?"

Meanwhile, Fetch made it to his knees, realized he was still hungry, so he crawled over to the refrigerator.

Cat watched his efforts with great amusement.

"What?" he asked.

"Oh, nothing. Just confirming a thought."

"What thought?"

She leveled a gaze at him. "As different species, I grudgingly have to admit there were never any conclusive proofs of the superiority of either of our respective species. But now, with both of us limited in this new form, the degree in which we adapted to this crisis proves what I knew all along."

"Huh?"

"Precisely my point," she sniffed.

"Fine, whatever," he sniffed, turning his attention to the big metal food box - refrigerator, his mind furnished the word to him. He stared at it.

Cat was digging at the kitchen window screen with quick movements.

Fetch stared at the refrigerator.

With a quick snatch, Cat captured whatever it was that had been trapped by the screen. A moth. She popped it into her mouth.

Fetch stared at the refrigerator.

"Blech," Cat said, spitting the still wriggling moth into the sink. "That was nasty. Weird, I usually like those." She turned and noticed Fetch's patient refrigerator vigilance. "What are you doing?"

"Waiting for food," he said, not willing to take his eyes from the source of food in case it appeared and he missed it.

"How's that working for you?"

"Not so well, but you just have to be patient."

"You have opposable thumbs," she noted.

Fetch tore his gaze from the source of pork chops. "Huh?"

Cat wiggled her thumbs. "These things. They allow you to grasp objects."

Fetch looked down at his paws ... hands ... and remembered he'd noticed them just a few moments ago. "Oh, yeah. I forgot about them."

Mimicking actions he'd seen Alpha make many times before, Fetch grabbed the handle of the refrigerator.

"It's working," he said delightedly as he grasped the handle.

"Now pull," Cat said, circling around the living room,

looking for warmth. A cool breeze was blowing through the broken window, bringing out goose pimples on her furless flesh. She eyed the television where she had spent countless afternoons sprawled on top drowsily soaking in electronic warmth. She picked up the remote and studied it, shivering.

Behind her, Fetch pulled the handle and the door swung open.

Tah-dah. Doggy Nirvana.

"Whoa!" he breathed, the refrigerator light bathing him in a halo of goodness He felt a phantom tail wagging.

Cheeses, meats, spaghetti, tomatoes (he liked tomatoes).

He drew in a deep breath before plunging into the wonders of...

Wait. There was nothing. No scent at all. All his twitching nose picked up was the feeling of coolness. There was no food smell at all.

It was so unfair. His non-existent tail stopped wagging.

And now the cold from the fridge combined with the chilliness circulating the room from the broken window started him shivering.

"Here," Cat said, draping a small blanket around him. He recognized it as the one from his doggy bed. The smell was familiar and comforting, though so faint he could barely pick it up. Why had he ever wanted to be a human? They can't smell anything, and without smells, the world was ... well... smell-less.

Phantom tail drooping, he closed the door, and headed over to the cabinet where he knew the good stuff was kept. Using his newfound powers of grasp-dom, he opened the cabinet door and beheld the sight of doggy treats in what he could see now was a brightly colored container.

"All right," he exulted. He grabbed the bag, rummaged it open, and shoved his face inside, trying in vain to reach the tantalizing nuggets just outside the reach of his flat face.

"Grrrr..."

He shoved his face deeper into the bag.

A pair of hands reached past him and pulled the bag away.

"What ...?" he started to say.

"Here, silly," she said, reaching a slim graceful hand into the bag. When she pulled it out, her hand was filled with crunchy goodness.

He lowered his head to gobble them up, but stopped when she poked him in the nose with her index finger.

"We're human now. I think. You should try and eat like a human."

"You mean with a spoon or fork," he asked, dismayed. He couldn't imagine shoving metal into his mouth.

"No, just take a piece like this," she delicately grabbed a piece between forefinger and thumb. "Then just put it in your mouth." She had no desire to try his food, so she held it out before his face.

Remembering his training with Alpha, Fetch knew better than to snatch at it. Slowly and carefully he brought his face up to her hand and gently took the piece into his mouth and swallowed it.

"Ow, that hurt," he said, grabbing his throat. Then the taste registered.

"Aack".

He tried spitting it out, but the food had already begun its meandering trip through his intestines.

"What's wrong," Cat asked, a wry smile playing across her face.

"That was horrible. I think there's something wrong with it. Maybe it went bad."

But wait. He liked food that went bad. Some of his favorite meals ever came from congealed slop scavenged from trash cans.

While he was thinking, Cat opened the refrigerator. She took out the milk carton and poured some into a shallow dish. Frowning, she studied the dish, deciding whether to just lick the milk from the container. Deciding not, she dipped her hand into the milk, capturing some in her palm. She raised her hand to her mouth and sucked up the milk.

"Not very efficient," she murmured., fastidiously wiping off the milk mustache.

The werewolf plummeting through space suddenly met something that wasn't space. It cried out as it crashed onto rocks and tumbled down the steep ravine.

Fetch's head whipped around, spraying food around. "What was that?"

Cat had taken some food out of the refrigerator and had put it in the microwave, a device she had taken to lying on at night after the human had gone to sleep. She had seen him heat food in it, and after some trial and error, she had successfully cooked a bag of sliced ham. That is, after a few minutes, the bag exploded, which she assumed meant it was ready. Ignoring the burnt odor, she'd put the melted plastic and steaming meat on the counter. Fetch had been going to town on it, gobbling it down, whimpering whenever he burnt himself.

Cat had heard the sound outside, too. It had been a cry of pain.

"Alpha," Fetch breathed.

Cat frowned. "It just sounded like a dog or something."

Fetch dropped the ham, hesitated, picked it up again and ran to the broken window. "It was Alpha. I know it was."

Cat joined him at the window. Fetch gave her a quick glance. Why did she look so good? Sleek, graceful with angular beauty. And why hadn't he ever noticed? Then another noise outside and his attention went back to the moonlit night. "We have to help him. He's in trouble!"

"I don't know," Cat said slowly. As long as she was fed and the litter was cleaned, she wasn't as attached to the human. Speaking of litter...

Meanwhile, Fetch was dancing around the window, carefully avoiding broken glass, some of which had found its way to the floor when the werewolf had jumped out. Most of the glass was undoubtedly outside. Fetch was mildly surprised he had reasoned that out.

He bounced over to Cat who was studying her litter box with a frown.

"We have to go! We have to go! We have to go!"

She looked up. "We?"

"Yes, we. He's Alpha! We have to protect Alpha!"

She shook her head slowly. "He's not my Alpha."

Fetch stopped bouncing. "Okay, maybe not for you. But it's important to me. If you won't come, I'll do it myself." He turned back to the window, ready to hurl himself through where the werewolf had disappeared.

Cat sighed, "Fine, I'll go with you."

"Really!? Yay! Let's go."

She looked down at her hands and shook her head. "No, not yet. I'm not going anywhere without claws."

The werewolf bounced and tumbled down the ravine, crying out at each jolting blow. Then his head slammed against a boulder and consciousness flew away.

Fetch watched carefully as Cat taped a serrated steak knife

to her forefinger, wrapping the tape around the handle of the knife and her newfound dexterous finger. When she was done, she critically examined the result and waggled the fingers. Knives were taped to each of the fingers and thumb of her right hand. "This isn't very comfortable," she muttered.

"Do you want me to do the other hand?" Fetch asked.

She sighed. "I don't know. I might just make do with this."

"Can we go?" Fetch said.

Cat sighed. "We might as well."

"All right!"

Fetch ran for the back door and skidded to a stop. He stared at the door.

"Thumbs," Cat reminded him.

Fetch jerked. "Oh, that's right, I forgot."

He grabbed the latch and pulled it open the way he'd known Alpha to do. The door obediently slid open.

Now what?

Usually when Alpha opened the door, Fetch would rush into the back yard, nose on overdrive, ready to hassle any cat or wildlife that had dared venture onto his domain.

But the gloom and darkness seemed pregnant with... something. He sniffed deeply, his senses letting him down. There was no rich banquet of scents riding the air molecules. Instead, woefully inadequate filtered, mixed and muted smells barely registered on his senses. And his newfound human sight, though improved in clarity and color, were barely useful in the moon-dappled shadows.

"I can't see very well," Cat said, sliding next to him.

Fetch woofed in surprise. He hadn't heard her approach.

"I can't smell anything," he said.

"I can't see very well," she complained.

"And my hearing..."

"...sucks, right?" she completed.

He nodded.

Cat sighed. "Like I said, and they think they're the second top species in the world?"

Fetch shot her a glance, "Second? Second to what?"

"Cats, of course."

"I dunno about that," he said slowly. "Why wouldn't dogs be up there?"

Amusement glinted in her eyes. "Seriously?"

He glared down at her." Yes, seriously. Wolf packs have ruled the plains and forests forever."

"Oh?"

"Yeah, where do you think that phrase 'top dog' came from? We're the top, baby."

"And would you consider the wolf your top dog?'

He put hands on his hips. "Yes."

"So if we took your 'top dog'" she mimed finger quotes, ", a wolf, against the top cat, what do you think would happen?"

"Um, the wolf would..."

"Run for his life," she interrupted.

"No way!"

"Yes way. Come here." She took his arm, and dragged him over to a book case, where several years of National Geographic magazines were stacked. Studying the magazines for a moment, she pulled one out and flipped through the pages, careful not to shred its pages with the knives strapped to her fingers. When she found what she wanted, she grinned, and handed him the magazine.

"That's our top cat."

Fetch gasped. It was a picture of an orange striped cat mauling an antelope. The deer was dwarfed by the enormous tiger, which was biting its neck and raking huge claws down the antelope's side. The deer's mouth was open in silent agony and terror.

"And this," Cat said, plopping another magazine into his hands.

A pride of lions bringing down a bellowing Cape Buffalo.

"We're killers," Cat said matter-of-factly. "It's what we do. I kill anything that I can. Bugs, spiders, mice, rabbits. It doesn't matter if I'm hungry or not. I kill it. I might play with it first, but then I'll kill it."

Fetch's mouth dropped open.

Cat noticed his look of horror and shrugged. "You dogs aren't that way. You kill when you're hungry or defending something. We kill because we're killers."

"But, but..."

"You're just lucky you're too big to be my prey," she said, crossing back to the open door.

Fetch could have sworn he saw a quick smile.

As Fetch followed Cat to the door, he reflected that there was another disadvantage to being human. As a dog, his thoughts rarely expanded beyond food, comfort, companionship and play. But as a human, he found himself wondering about things, hurting his brain rather than learning the truth by simply sniffing something's butt.

He looked at Cat's swaying nude rear end exposed under her blanket as she strode towards the door. Conflicting emotions roiled inside him.

She looked over her shoulder and caught him looking. "You aren't going to sniff my butt... or anything else of mine."

"I wasn't..."

"Yes, you were. You were thinking about sniffing my butt."

"Well, okay, maybe. But why not? I mean, don't you sniff butts?"

She grimaced. "Cats don't sniff butts."

"What? You don't want to sniff my butt?"

Her nose crinkled, "No thanks, I can smell it from here."

"No you can't!"

"You're right. I can't. But it doesn't mean I want to."

"Then how else can you learn the truth about stuff? You can learn about something's health, sex, mood, intentions, just by smelling."

"I don't need any of that. Like I said, I just kill everything. Then I go lay in a sunbeam until it's time to eat."

"Yeah, I like sunbeams," Fetch agreed. "And eating."

He caught up with Cat as she stood in the doorway, staring into the darkness and flexing her clawed hand. "You weren't serious about killing me, were you?"

She just smiled.

After an awkward moment of staring into the woods surrounding the house, he said, "We have to go after Alpha."

He was feeling strange. While his still tremendous sense of loyalty made him want to run and search for Alpha, something else made him hesitate, a feeling that all was not right with Alpha, and that there was something going on that he would be better off not knowing. He'd never felt anything that countered his sense of pack loyalty, and he didn't like the feeling.

But in the end, loyalty won out. Loyalties always win out with a dog. That's why a dog will sit for days next to its dead owner. It's why a dog will travel hundreds of miles to find its way home. It's why a dog will defend its family or pack, against any intruder, no matter the odds.

He took a deep breath, and stepped into the cold dark, drawing his blanket around him as the chill hit him. He felt rather than heard as Cat followed him into the dark.

The werewolf shook its head groggily. He was laying on a smattering of loose rocks and boulders at the bottom of a ravine next to a small brook. He ignored the pleasant sound of water whooshing into swirling eddies and small pools, eroding rock with mindless, endless patience He snarled softly, protesting the pain in his head, and shook himself to his feet.

He stood by the stream, swaying slightly as his body sought to regain its physical equilibrium. Mentally, less adjustment was necessary. In werewolf form, his thoughts were almost overwhelmed with red-colored rage and hunger. Real cognitive thought was fleeting and elusive. No memories to speak of. Just the need to outrace pain and hunger, ripping, tearing, rending anything unfortunate enough to cross his path. It was why they could consider humans as prey. Werewolves were no longer human. Nor were they true wolves with a rich complexity of pack family. They were something else. If they ran into another werewolf, chances were even that they would rip each other to shreds or join together in a one night only pack. Hungry or not, they would kill anything they saw. Mindless attacks that didn't kill would often create a new werewolf. Some who survived a werewolf attack believed that the fortunate people were the ones who didn't survive. Others reveled in the change.

Fetch searched through the grass, keeping a wary distance from broken glass. He puffed out an exasperated snort. "I can't pick up a scent."

Cat ignored him, studying the dirt at the edge of the lawn. "It went through here."

Fetch looked up. "How do you know that?"

She pointed, "You can see the tracks from its passage."

Fetch's eyebrows went up. "You can?" He trotted over and looked down.

Cat took a few more steps and pointed into the woods. "See, it ran up here, and went that way."

"Weird. It's like a smell track, but visual instead. I didn't think anything like that was possible. Maybe humans aren't as sensory-deprived as I thought." He frowned. Sensory-deprived? Where had that thought come from? Boy, humans were smart.

Cat was oblivious to his ruminations, and was tracking where the werewolf had entered the woods, following prints illuminated by sunlight bounced off the moon's surface.

The werewolf was back in motion. It had scrabbled up the

ravine and was now racing through the woods. Where was that deer that had eluded him? Where was anything else? Must kill. Must chase.

A raccoon saw it coming and frantically scampered up a tree. The werewolf barely spared it a glance, its hunting senses telling it the raccoon would be too difficult to catch once it gained the branches. So the werewolf headed back the way it had come, searching for easier prey.

"Now what?" Fetch asked.

The tracks ended abruptly at a small, slow moving river.

"I think it swam through here." Cat looked up and down the bank, hoping to see the tracks taking a wiser course. But it seemed pretty clear that the werewolf had gone into the river. She sighed.

"Okay, we swim," Fetch said. "I like swimming."

"I hate swimming," Cat groused.

"Too bad," Fetch said. While following the werewolf tracks he had warmed and now that the dark didn't seem so intimidating, he was getting into the spirit of the chase. Dogs hunted in this manner, and it felt good to be following his lifetime instincts. Even better that Cat had joined the hunt.

He looped the blanket around his neck, and stepped into the water. "Whoa, it feels weird on my bare skin. And cold."

Cat looked unhappy.

When Fetch hit deeper water, he launched forward, dog-paddling furiously. His new form seemed more adaptable to the water, his hands efficiently pulling him through the water, while his legs kicked less effectively. In just minutes, he was across. Shivering, he climbed onto the far bank. He wrapped the blanket tightly around himself, and looked back at Cat. She was chewing her lip, staring into the black water.

"You can do it," Fetch urged.

She ignored him with cat aplomb.

Fetch grinned. "Here kitty, kitty, kitty."

Cat's head whipped up and she snarled.

Fetch's grin widened. "Oh, wait. Sorry, it's not smart to pick on a killer, right?"

At that, Cat slipped into the water, and started swimming awkwardly across. It was the first time ever he had seen her anything other than graceful.

As she got closer to the bank, he snorted happily. "Hey, what are you doing?"

"Swimming," she said, doing her best to keep her face just above the water, knives slicing ineffectively through the liquid.

"Hah, no, you're not. You're dog-paddling!"

"I most certainly am not," she growled, feet searching for the bottom.

"Oh, yeah, then what do you call it?"

"Cat-paddling," she said, no hint of humor on her face as she reached the shallows, wrapping the blanket around her as she climbed the bank.

Suddenly, a howl came from the woods at the top of the bluff. Cat stiffened. If she had still had her tail, it would have been poofed.

Fetch frowned, "Weird. I don't understand that dialect."

There was another howl, punctuated by a crashing through underbrush.

"It's getting closer," Fetch said. Something bubbled up in his throat. "Hey! Hey! Hey!"

Cat frowned at him. "What are you doing?"

"I'm barking."

"That's not barking."

"Sure it is. Hey! Hey!"

He paused. "Hmmm, you're right."

The noise from the woods was closer. Something was storming towards them with berserker speed.

"We need to go," Cat staid nervously. She started towards the trees, her intent to climb as fast and as high as she could. She'd worry about getting down later.

Before they could gain safety, something black and monstrous erupted from the trees, glaring at them with maddened eyes.

"A-A-Alpha?" Fetch stammered.

The werewolf snarled, tongue licking fangs.

"Come on," Cat cried, grabbing Fetch's arm, running down the riverbank.

Fetch resisted for a moment, but then the werewolf burst into chase, and Fetch started running.

The werewolf exulted in the chase, bloodlust driving rational thought from its brain.

The boy and girl sprinted as fast as they could, stumbling over the uneven ground.

Fetch looked back and gasped, "Why are we running? It's Alpha."

"No, it's not," Cat said, yanking him forward. She eyed the water, but didn't know if their pursuer was an even more efficient swimmer than them. She would save the river for a last resort.

But the werewolf was silently gaining yards on them every few seconds, its bounding leaps gobbling up the distance separating them. It gained ground much more quickly than Cat realized, and then it pounced.

Huge paws slammed them to the ground.

They crumpled in agony as bones began to yield.

Ben Herdt woke covered in dew. He groaned.

His head hurt. His body was a mass of agony.

What had happened?

A weak sun was building up strength and burning off the night's coolness and as the sensations of being cold, wet and naked sunk in, he realized what had happened and groaned again, this time in recognition of his stupidity. How had he forgotten last night was the full moon? He had been running right under its full face, not realizing what it portended for him. He'd just been so distracted by his horrible day at the office. He vowed to set up a system to remind him in the future. Just one more thing to think about as a new werewolf.

Though he knew it was hopeless, still he looked around for

his Montrail Melees running shoes. They were expensive, but worse than the cost would be the hassle of breaking in a new pair.

And that's when he saw them.

Two bodies spread out on the sparkly dew covered bank next to him. He reached out a hand.

As he felt the well-known and beloved touch of his Alpha, Fetch sighed with pleasure and leaned into the caress. Then scary barely remembered memories went through his brain and he snorted awake, scrambling to his feet.

"Wuff?"

"Hey, boy," Herdt said. He looked around and noticed Cat motionless on the grass. He leaned towards her and Cat's eyes shot open. In an instant she was on her feet, hyper alert and ready to dart in any direction.

"It's okay," Herdt said, reaching a hand to stroke her fur. Warily she stepped just outside his reach, but didn't run away. He grinned. Typical cat contrariness.

But that didn't explain what they were doing out here. He wished they could answer, but they were just animals. There was a blanket on the ground. He looked further downriver where another lay half submerged in the water.

Examining the first blanket, he realized it was one of his own.

"Even more weird," he murmured.

He wrapped the blanket around his torso, scooped Cat up before she could object, and patted Fetch who was trying to get a nose under his hand. "C'mon, boy."

As Herdt headed downriver to get the other blanket, he wondered about being werewolf and what it might bring next. And he mulled over the surprise of his pets somehow having found him.

He had no idea their next surprise would be a doozy ... when the next full moon came out.

I hope you enjoyed this short story. MOONED has now been published as a full-length novel.

~ Norm

Moo-ving Experiences

by Kathleen C. Z. Klevorn

D r. Pacho grew up in the South American country of Colombia, spending much of his time in the city of Bogota, the capital and largest city in the country. Two unique experiences during his childhood helped him make his career choice and others have reinforced that decision to become a veterinarian---and not a professional soccer player.

The first experience that helped him to decide that he wanted to be a veterinarian were his weekend trips to his father's farm. On Fridays, he traveled to his dad's farm, where there were all types of domestic animals: horses, cows, goats, chickens, pigs, sheep, ducks, turkeys, geese, dogs and cats. It was like heaven for a young boy who was developing a love of animals and nature. He

cherished spending time there with his father and his animals. His days were spent running up and down the hills, eating wild berries, jumping in the river, chasing animals, and helping with the farm chores. It was a nice break from the busy life of the city in Bogota. There were so many things that he could do on the farm without an adult holding his hand, that he couldn't do in the city. He wandered around the farm on his own, played with his toys in the dirt, and developed a real sense of independence.

The second experience that led young Pacho to pursue veterinary medicine occurred sometime between the age of nine and twelve. His maternal grandfather came to his house in Bogota with two rabbits, three guinea pigs, some food for them and a book about how to raise them. He told Pacho to read the book, learn how to breed them and then sell them for their meat because many  restaurants in Colombia serve rabbit and guinea pig meat. This seemed like the perfect job for him because he had some experience being around animals. Caring for the animals and then selling them taught him the difference between companion animals and production animals, a concept that would be important when it came time to choose a career focus.

His business went very well and expanded to the point that he had to take the animals to his father's farm when he was about fifteen years old, for lack of space on the patio in their city home. It also started to become difficult to have enough time for the business because of his school work and the time he spent playing soccer. He had dreams of becoming a professional soccer player which made the sport hard to give up. Ultimately, his mother told him that she didn't want him to be a soccer player and to try something else. This prompted him to start researching a career with animals. "I learned very quickly that veterinary medicine is versatile. As a veterinarian, I could work in public policy, with small animals, in a laboratory, a zoo, or with production animals." He decided to explore this path.

In Colombia, high school ends after eleventh grade and there is no undergraduate degree requirement for veterinary medicine, so he went straight into vet school when he was seventeen. At this point, he became even busier with school and just couldn't take care of the animals anymore. He was able to sell all of them to the farmers and farm workers at the neighboring farms.

After the five-year vet school program, Pacho practiced for two years in Colombia while also working on his master's degree. He had two very different experiences during this time. He loved the large animal environment and helping on the farms in the area. The farmers seemed to better understand that animals are like humans in that they sometimes die, and it can be cruel to keep them alive. They had a saying, "Livestock, Deadstock". Livestock farmers are aware of the limitations to provide extensive health care to animals in the field. Even though farmers are very attached to their animals, they won't let them suffer for unnecessary reasons.

This contrasted with his experiences with small animal owners in a small animal hospital. There was a lot of pressure from clients to do things to care for their pets when it was not in the best interest of the animal. He did not appreciate the drama and difficulty in dealing with these sorts of clients. Most of the time, there are no monetary restrictions for small animal owners and they may expose the animals to unnecessary treatments or pain just to keep them around longer. These measures increase the stress among veterinarians, technicians and owners. After this experience, he was sure of his decision to focus his career on large animals.

In 2011, he moved to the United States to pursue a doctoral program in animal science. He landed at Cornell University in Ithaca, New York. During the time that he has been in Ithaca, he has continued to work in ambulatory medicine. He loves visiting the farms to care for the animals and getting to know the owners and their farm workers. He compares what he does today to the book All Creatures Great and Small, by James Herriot. The calls he makes today are the same type that the Yorkshire veterinarian, Dr. Herriot, made in England decades ago when the book was written. He calls this book a "must read" for every veterinarian.

Pacho has had many challenges over the years treating large animals. At first, he had calls to care for cows, horses, pigs, goats, sheep, alpaca and even some water buffalo. The owners of the water buffalo eventually realized that Ithaca was not the right environment for them and sent them to Texas, a much better climate for them. He once worked on a swine farm for a month while he was in vet school and couldn't stand the piglets screaming. When he would go home and try to sleep at night, he would still hear them screaming. It was obvious that pigs were not the right animal for him.

When it came time to specialize in one type of large animal, he realized that working with cattle was his true passion. He loves the cows, and they love him. It's like having thousands of pets when he is visiting the large dairy farms. They run around him, chase him and come up to lick him. Somehow, they know that he is their friend and they trust him. He spends his days checking cows to see if they are pregnant, with his arms inside the cattle to his elbow, performing surgeries, and treating and preventing diseases. It's a physically exhausting job, but he loves the work and is always learning more about these amazing animals. Pacho says, "I am amazed at a cow's resistance to pain. I was doing abdominal surgery on a cow once and we only use local anesthesia in the field. This cow was still eating from the beginning of the surgery until the end."

Some may question his decision to become a production veterinarian instead of a veterinarian for companion animals, like cats and dogs. All of his life experiences made it easy for him to understand that we domesticate some animals to provide companions and some to provide food for the growing human population. Veterinarians, like Pacho, work every day to provide the best living conditions for production animals, something he learned very early in his life, when he got the rabbits and guinea pigs from his grandfather. There is a famous quote from Dr. Temple Grandin: "I think using animals for food is an  ethical thing to do, but we've got to do it right. We've got to give those animals a decent life and we've got to give them a painless death. We owe the animal respect." Pacho follows this principle in his practice.

There is one particular story that stands out in his mind. One day the ambulatory department received a call from a distraught dairy farmer whose cow was having difficulty calving. Pacho was not working that day and had a full day planned with research and studying. No one else in the department was available, so they asked Pacho to go. He really didn't want to go. He was busy and had too much to do, but he got in his truck and left Ithaca.

While he was driving to the farm that was almost an hour away, he was thinking, "I don't have time for this. Calving can take minutes or hours. I could be gone all day and get nothing else done." The call had put him in a bad mood.

When he arrived at the farm, his mood totally changed. He saw how upset the farmer was. The farmer told Pacho that he had lost a family member the night before and that he hadn't slept much. Then, he found out that his cow was in labor and in danger of not making it through calving. It put Pacho's bad mood into perspective.

After several hours, Pacho was able to perform a successful cesarean section and deliver the heifer alive while saving the mother as well. The farmer was so grateful. It's one of the happiest stories in his memory that didn't start out that way. Delivering the calf turned a bad day into a good day for all parties involved and became one of Pacho's most moo-ving experiences in his career so far.

When he finished his Ph.D. degree in 2018, Dr. Pacho was offered a Clinical Instructor position in the ambulatory department of the vet school at Cornell. He has been teaching students, conducting clinical research, and serving the dairy farms in the area for the past two years. A different moo-ving  experience is on the horizon for him as a tenure track Assistant Professor at Washington State University in Pullman, Washington. The cattle and dairy farmers there will provide new stories for the next chapter of Dr. Pacho's adventures.

A Different Kind of Animal

by Diane Perry

What was then so far away,
Is pandemic here today,
Anxiety brings tears
Panic intensifies fears.

Squirt, squirt, splash, is the sanitizer on my hands,
And snap, pull, snap, is my N-95 duck mask.

Discouraging long plane trips,
Quarantine to a cruise ship,
Fever, cough and shortness of breath,
And no vaccine can mean death.

What started in China,
Has spread like a wildfire,
Caused by civets, pangolins and bats,
Yet nothing truly proves any of that.

First thought on a ship was SARS or norovirus
But learned of something else, called Coronavirus.

Time to buy soap and toilet paper needs,
And stock up on can corn, carrots, and beans,
Need to be safe and quarantine,
If exposed to COVID-19.

A Canine's Healing Journey

by Jolee L. Price

Animals are a big part of my life; always have been and always will be, so it was to my delight when my husband mentioned getting another dog. The word "yes" roared emphatically in my mind, I thought it was audible.

The next day he came home from errands and asked me if I wanted to go to the shelter. I didn't need to be asked twice. I was ready to go in minutes.

We saw many male dogs and puppies and a few females. There were two dogs we were interested in – a four-month old beagle mix, and a hound dog named "Mama." The paper on her cage said she was two, but a lady there told us more likely between four and five. She was rescued from being euthanized while pregnant. We were told the dog's real name was not known and when a pregnant cat or dog is brought in, the workers and/or volunteers call them "Mama Kitty or Mama Dog."

There was such sadness in her eyes, which were literally clouded over. I thought she had cataracts. To me, her look told me she was ready to give up. Her physical appearance conveyed she had been through a lot. We adopted her on the spot.

Adapting with any new pet takes time; more when abuse and neglect are involved. There's no actual timetable on healing and trust; it's step-by-step and day-by-day.

Her gamey scent was pungent, and a bath was needed. We were told at the shelter that Big "R" now known as Stock + Field, had a room where you can wash your pets yourself. Her grayish fur became white. Upon closer examination, several scars were visible evidencing physical abuse. When we would pet her, she would stare at our hand and literally cower. Her cowering response was the same with loud noises and raised voices. When called, she came ever so slowly, with her head down and tail between her legs. There were times her head was bowed so low, I thought her snout was dragging on the floor.

Even picking up branches in our yard affected her. I was picking up branches in our back yard, and I went to pass her. She sat frozen in place, fixated on the branch in my hand. It didn't take the mind of Einstein to figure out that scenario. I slowly lowered the branch, ignored her and walked to our yard waste container.

We took Mama to our vet for an examination. She needed to be spayed due to her teats (nipples) lightly grazing the ground due to apparently many litters. An oral exam of her mouth revealed a dental procedure would be needed due to several fractured teeth. And then, her in-house Heart worm test came back positive.

We were told two injections of arsenic, one at a time, with much observation and rest, would need to be done to kill the heart worms. My husband and I wanted to discuss and pray about her treatment before deciding. In the interim, she was given heart worm medicine.

A few days later, we picked up a CD with her heart x-ray on it to take to another vet regarding the heart worm issue. Furthermore, per our own vet's phone call to us, Mama's stool result showed tapeworm, whip worm and coccidia, which is an intestinal parasite that mostly causes watery, mucus-based diarrhea in dogs, and if not treated, over time it can cause damage to the lining of the dog's intestinal tract.

She was on a lot of medicine. Our kitchen counter looked like a pharmaceutical shelf. She threw up a few times. We were told worms come out by vomit and poop. I took her to the vet where she was given one shot for nausea and one shot for a rash on one of her teats. I then had to put cortisone not only on all her teats but on a hemorrhoid as well. We continued to pray for guidance and direction.

Within a few weeks, she was doing better and was becoming a shadow to our other dog. She even gave me her first "doggie" kiss. She licked my left hand twice. God Bless her heart I thought. It was my hope she was beginning to trust us. I thanked God, Jesus and the Holy Spirit!

During this whole time, my husband and I prayed for her. We also laid hands on her and prayed for her. I envisioned reaching inside her heart, grabbing the heart worms and crushing them in my bare hands killing them all.

I can't explain it, but one day I had peace about her. I knew that I knew that I knew she was healed of heart worm. I told my husband why I wanted a second heart worm test, and he agreed. I made an appointment which was two months and one day after we adopted her. She had a great checkup. Her blood work was excellent, and the re-check on the heart worm test was a weak positive. Another sample was taken to be sent out; with the results coming back the next day. The vet told me he never saw a false/positive before, and I told him that I had a false/positive regarding pregnancy before so it can happen. My husband and I prayed and commanded that heart worm test to be negative in the Name of Jesus, Amen. We didn't want our dog to get arsenic injections.

The next day the vet called and said the testing sent out to the lab they dealt with yesterday confirmed NO HEART WORM!!! He called it a miracle. I told him it was God; that praying to God, love and good food helped, and he agreed. He again called it a miracle but wanted to check her again in six months. Of course, that test and others since have been negative. Praise God!

I immediately told my husband the good news, and he said, "What did you expect?" He is right. We are to expect good things from God.

Once her heart issue was cleared, she then had her dental procedure, which included one major and three minor extractions.

Once recovered from that procedure, she was spayed.

It's been over three years since we adopted her. She's come

a long way both physically and emotionally. Cloudiness from her eyes disappeared, and her white fur glistens. Her teats shrunk considerably and no longer graze the ground.

Abuse of any kind is evil and should not be tolerated.

I know not all, whether human or animal, are healed. I don't know why, but I do know I will not question a Blessing.

Some may reason the validity of the testing. My husband and I don't. If we did, where is our faith and belief?

Ode to Otis

by Jeanne Meeks

an's best friend is not my best friend. The first time I met Otis, he attacked the front door as if we were criminals rather than grandparents coming to visit. At sixty pounds, he could easily knock me over with a twist of his body, a pit bull from the look of him.

My son and family have big hearts and love their dogs. They spoiled their last pet, Clark, a fourteen-year-old dachshund. He had been Barb's baby since before our grandsons, Sean and Wyatt, were born. Clark's death left the family lonely and incomplete.

Six months later, the four of them visited an animal shelter on a whim. Rows of enclosures held playful little dogs, friendly mutts, and even a sleek young dachshund. The boys went from cage to cage, tickled by the attention given to them by exciting dogs.

Brian kept going back to the last cage. "Barb, look at this one."

A big brute sat in the back corner of his cage with his massive head hung low. A pit bull/boxer mix, the staff guessed. His wide jaws were made for clamping down on a rope or stick or a leg. Yet, his big sad eyes would not make contact. He turned away.

"Come here, poor baby. Come here." Barb coaxed him with her sweet voice.

Rescue dogs have often been abused and come with baggage. The shelter's vet suspected this one had been used as a bait dog in the fighting ring. The fierce-looking dog finally crept forward, low on his haunches. He allowed their strange hands to scratch and pet him. Starved for love, he ducked his head under Brian's hand to be petted. Knowing the breed's reputation for viciousness, Barb and Brian introduced the dog to their sons carefully. The boys were shy too.

"Let him sniff your hand. Reach out slowly." Brian knelt next to Sean, ready to intervene.

Sean understood, and his gentle nature soon won the dog over. Five-year-old Wyatt made him flinch and duck, but the two worked it out under their father's watchful eye. After an hour of getting to know each other, the pit bull stole the family's hearts.

They named him Otis Day for no particular reason other than my son has a sense of humor and loved the movie Animal House as a kid. Otis wasn't a good house guest. His new parents could take no chances with the unpredictable dog and their two boys. He ate socks and burst every ball in the house. Stuffed animals didn't stand a chance.

Otis was to be caged at night but chewed his way out every time. He finally learned to sleep in the cage, as long as the door was open. During the day, if the family was gone, Otis left gifts on the floor in odd places. Maybe he resented being left alone. It took a year for him to be house-trained by confining him to the large laundry room while they were gone.

In his first year with the family, they visited us at our lake house. Otis, the sixty-pound baby, kept trying to crawl into Barb's lap. Something scared him: the extra people, the water, boats going by. She hugged and reassured him and told him everything was okay. He repaid her by piddling in her lap. She took it in stride. Later, as we sat in a circle in the grass at the edge of the beach talking and laughing, Otis sidled up to Barb and lifted his leg on her shoulder, twice. Barb is a kind and wonderful person.

While we sat on the beach, our grandsons played in the shallow water near shore. Wyatt wore his life jacket and laughed and splashed. Otis was beside himself. He paced the waterline, watching and worried. Finally, he couldn't take it any longer and swam out to grab Wyatt by the seat of his pants. He dragged the boy to safety, again and again.

My granddaughter refused to bring her tiny Havanese dog into the same house as Otis, afraid he'd eat the little guy. One bite and Frankie would be a goner. None of us could guarantee that wouldn't happen if Frankie darted through the room and Otis took chase. They've never met.

I kept my distance from Otis, as I do with most dogs. I like dogs when they lay at your feet in front of the fireplace or herd sheep or help in the hunt. I don't like those who jump up, slobber, or sniff at me. Somehow Otis knew. He'd sneak under the table and lay his chin on my knee, waiting for me to scratch his head. He worked to win me over and I gave in.

My brother-in-law, Bob, has two dogs and loves them like children. When he visited, he fussed over and played with Otis. Bob's a biker and wears a chain on his belt loop attached to his wallet. When he stood to leave, the chains rattled. Otis jumped away and bared his teeth with a menacing growl, ready to attack, scaring everyone. We figure chains were used to abuse him as a puppy.

A burglar would be insane to bother with my son's house. Otis was always the first one to the door to investigate. My son is frequently away on business but could rely on the pit bull to safeguard the family. Any odd sound from outside brought Otis to the window. His bark and menacing growl warned strangers he was on duty. When the boys left the house to play in the front yard, Otis forced himself out of the door and stationed himself between them and the busy road. In the backyard, he pretended to sleep in the shade but knew every move the boys made.

After several years, I knew Otis's worth. His life's work was to protect my son's home and my grandsons. His love, protection, and fierce loyalty belonged to them. As he matured, he asked little in return: to follow them around, a bone to gnaw on, to lay at their side. I sensed he would sacrifice his life for them. He became a dog to admire.

In early 2020 the family noticed the four-year-old dog wasn't himself. Otis's energy and personality were gone. His eyes lost their sparkle. He ignored the doorbell and wandered the house alone. He whined in pain.

A fast-growing tumor behind his eye had taken over his brain. It would grow and destroy him from the inside. It would kill him. The tumor could be removed but would grow back within six months. Barb and Brian had to make a terrible decision, to watch him die inch by inch or let him go quickly.

The vet had one suggestion. Researchers at the veterinary hospital at Purdue University in Indiana had notified all veterinaries of their search for patients with Otis's rare type of tumor. The same sort of tumor afflicted John McCain. The best surgeons had removed the senator's tumor, but it grew back quickly and killed him. Researchers searched for a cure ever since. The prospect of testing their experimental vaccine on a living patient excited them. Otis was the perfect subject because he was young and otherwise healthy. The university offered to do the surgery for free.

The odds were not good. Brian and Barb wrestled with the decision of putting Otis through the surgery, driving three hours back and forth to Indianapolis for months, and prolonging their worry and grief, only to have their poor dog die anyway. Yet, the vaccine the researchers hoped to develop would save human lives. It would prevent brain tumors from growing back once removed. That slim hope of helping human patients caused Barb to agree to subject her darling Otis to the surgery. She drove him to Perdue and gave him one last hug.

Barb and Brian gathered their sons to discussed the meaning of death. All their grandparents are still alive and the family had not suffered the pain of death. Sean, at twelve, understood the circle-of-life well enough. His nine-year-old brother nodded as Barb explained that all things are born, live, get old, and then pass away.

Then a realization hit. Wyatt cried out, "Do you mean Grandma Jeannie is going to die!"

The sweetheart had to call me to confirm I was still alive and would likely have many years left on earth. I cried too when I heard his worries.

Otis got through the surgery very well. The relief I felt when hearing the news amazed me. That big oaf of a dog had wormed his way into my emotions with his gentle nature and devotion to my grandchildren.

A week later Otis came home to a joyous family. He was groggy and thin. His head was shaved and stained orange with iodine around the incision. He was happy to be home but needed time to recuperate. His raucous playmates, Wyatt and Sean, sat with him, petted him gently, and let him mend.

The following week, Otis and Barb returned to Purdue for the experimental vaccine injection. She was to watch for odd behavior at home and return to the hospital each week for monitoring. Bringing Otis to the doctor became part of the family routine for six months. He would then be in the clear.

In the fourth week after surgery, Otis stumbled. He wasn't himself. He wandered and became listless. Our hopes faded. This is what the researchers had warned. Still, it was a shock.

Barb and Brian rushed Otis to the vet to hear what they already suspected. The fast-growing tumor had returned. The vaccine had failed. They took Otis back home to live out his days in the care of his family. It didn't take long. Otis had a massive seizure one night and died while the boys slept.

An Alabama research hospital which had been working with Perdue University asked for Otis's body. As painful as it was, the family let him go again. Barb and Brian wanted his death to mean something, to help people and save lives.

The next morning, Otis was gone and the children were informed. They held a family ceremony to remember their faithful friend. Still, a few days later, Wyatt asked, "When's Otis coming home?"

Loss is a lonely experience. We all grieve in different ways. Some shut out memory and let feelings fade. Others dwell in the pain. The most fortunate live and laugh in the memories of their passed loved ones.

My family chose to honor Otis by rescuing another dog. On their first visit to the animal shelter, they met an Otis look-alike. The pit bull had been recovering in the shelter for three months. Brian opted to call him Cash, a nod to the cost of adoption. He was outvoted. The new family member is named Jax, after the hero of a television series. Brian tells me Jax is calm, house-trained, and doing his part to fill a gaping hole.

I haven't met Jax yet, but if he protects my grandchildren and has the heart and devotion Otis had, I'll give him a chance. I'm not an animal lover but admit there are a few rare exceptions.

Ode to Otis

Clamping jaws may snap and break bones in two.

His massive head cocked to listen and claws

at the ready to tear and savage on cue.

Sleek muscles quiver and tense, but pause.

Sad doleful eyes speak otherwise.

Their kindness brings the brute to his knees

To beg for a master and place to be.

He'd protect in fealty, alert to their cries,

Fierce in danger, his mission to please

the humans who chose him, his family.

Animals of the Jungle

by Lenny Kapocius

I n May, 1944, on Manus, the bombardment and fighting had almost secured the island. We still had rifles and ammunition handy. We were given clean Marine fatigues and we dumped the close we wore for 33 days while we traveled on the ocean. Then, when time permitted, we walked with others up to higher ground on a hill nearby for some breeze. The temperature was 115°. The animals in the jungle suffered.

As the coconut, palm, and banana trees, along with the rest of the beautiful tropical growth, had been shredded to pieces from the bombardment during the invasion, the Koala bears fell from their tree nests. The ground animals were in complete disarray.

I picked up two little orphan pigs, but I had no means to help them. They squeaked so loud, two natives heard it. They came out of the jungle and gladly took them from me.

Then there were the bats. They only flew at night. Their bodies grew to about three pounds and the natives ate their meat.

When two young native boys saw that Perry and I carried a rifle, they came out of the jungle quickly and followed us. We stopped and sat on a log next to a wide area of sandy land. The 10-year-old, Pomumu, was very conversant in his own Polynesian language. He blabbed the same words over and over with hand motions aiming toward the tree tops.

We finally got the message. He wanted us to shoot some bats down for him. For food, he explained.

How does one do that? One shot from a rifle would ring so loud through the jungle that it would scare all the bats to another area.

Pomumu motioned to us. "Wait, I will be right back." He came back and set the stage.

He brought a couple of dead snakes and plopped them down in the center of the wide area of sand we sat next to. Then we waited. After thirty minutes, the snakes swelled from the heat of the sun, which radiated a signal to the bath up high in the trees that there was food below.

The bats awoke and swooped down for the food. My buddy, Perry, the better rifleman, used his carbine and shot three bats as they got close to picking up the snakes.

The larger one was about four pounds, with a wingspan of six feet, and the two smaller ones each weighed about two pounds.

These two native boys thanked us for the bats as they carried them away and walked into the jungle.

Weeks after things were organized, we had some spare time to explore with some restrictions. I found a parrot that liked me. Some fortunate one took it home after the war ended.

The Myna Bird

A lady and man who I was acquainted with had this large tropical bird. It screeched loud as ever whenever someone appeared on site. It was caged in a room which accessed the tavern they owned. The room also had a private entrance to access for family and close friends.

Barney the bird repeated, loud and clear as ever, everything he heard sooner or later. It learned some bad words from tavern customers. John the bartender occasionally placed Barney in his cage in a corner way back in the tavern, almost out of sight. When a customer came through the tavern door, we could only guess what Barney would shout out loudly.

Once, two ladies – first-time customers – entered the tavern. With the door not yet closed behind them, Barney shouted out loud, "Wow, look who just came in."

Those two ladies were flabbergasted and John had to do

some explaining to them.

Another time, a neatly dressed gentleman just sat down at the bar. Barney hollered loud as ever, "Hey Jack, no more mooching drinks. Get out of here and go find yourself a job."

The best kicker was so bad and insulting that John placed Barney with his cage in a back room of the tavern forever.

One day, one of John's distant relatives came to the tavern near closing time. As soon as she entered, Barney shouted loud as ever, "Here comes the old battle ax. I wish he stayed home."

That certainly was a short visit.

This would be my favorite way to become friendly with animals.

This little girl seems to have the right technique.

Essential Purification

by Dawn E. Plestina

I surround you, exist within you and without you, but you need me to survive. Travel with me to discover the beauty and diversity of this world. Observing nature allows us the opportunity to view without prejudice. Can one keep an open mind? That will be up to you, dear reader, to decide.

Ah, the stuff of fairy tales- Yellow-eyed Penguins from the shores of New Zealand! The species is known for being the least social of all penguins, but within their species they develop a strong bond during mating season. Building their nest together begins their monogamous relationship. After they copulate, and the female lays the eggs, both the male and female take turns foraging for food and protecting their chicks. After about three months, the chicks become fledglings and leave home which signals the end of the breeding season. Yellow-eyed Penguins return to their original mate in the fall and even to the same area to begin their bonding and breeding each year until one or both no longer live. A "happily ever after" ending, don't you agree?

As you join me in the Pacific Ocean, we find the Big-Belly Seahorse which is the largest of all seahorses and not any relation to Dr. Seuss' Star-bellied or Plain-bellied Sneeches, although there might be a similar moral by the end of this piece. Women may admire this species because of the mating routine. When a male inflates his abdomen, he is demonstrating that he is ready to mate. He sidles up to a female (who is always larger) and like a tandem bicycle ride, they swim together. During their swim, the female passes the eggs from her pouch to his. No need to reread, that is not a typo, but women may want to read it again and picture the father of their child doing the carrying and birthing.

Moving northwest, we find clownfish protecting and preserving the sea anemone. All clownfish are born male and will stay male if they are under pressure. One large female rules all of the males of a given sea anemone. (The stereotype of the nagging wife in many 1950's shows comes to mind.) Because the female clownfish harasses the males, they continue to feel stressed out and remain male. Stress releases the hormone, cortisol, which prevents males from turning female. The queen breeds with the alpha male. None of her offspring will take her place because the fry (newborns) will go with the current where they will turn into full-grown clownfish and find their own anemone.

The Yellow-eyed Penguin, the Big-Belly Seahorse, and clownfish are naturally occurring species within the animal kingdom. Humans do not tend to judge them, and yet, when humans happen to act in ways similar to these species, the judgement of others can be harsh.

People have reported bullying based on their sexual orientation going back decades. Since the late 1990's and the development of social media, all types of bullying have increased dramatically. Children have been bullied about their sexual orientation even in elementary school. Dr. Seuss' "The Sneetches" meant to teach young children not to judge one another based on looks ended with all Sneetches putting aside their differences and becoming friends with one another.

Perhaps the description of the Yellow-eyed Penguin felt the most comfortable to you, and so you made no judgement. What would happen if you came across a couple that caught your eye because something just didn't seem as you expected? When you realize the man is not holding hands with a woman, but rather, a man who is dressed like a woman, do you judge? Take the clownfish as another example. If you were introduced to a woman at a party and struck up a conversation which began a friendship, what would happen if later you found out that the woman was born a man?

Many people do not fit into our traditional male and female roles. They are ridiculed for not being normal. Take a moment to consider the three species again and each species' uniqueness. Would you call any of those abnormal? Or do you accept them because they are part of the beauty and diversity of this world.

Who am I to ask you to consider your views? I am the salt of the sea and land. I am the salt that keeps you alive and purifies you. I do not judge; I allow life to continue, and I appreciate all life. I hope you join me in appreciating the beauty and diversity of all life- no matter what form it takes.

My Big Sister

by Diane Perry

When my cat of nineteen years passed away, my heart felt so empty. My home was too quiet and I missed the pitter-patter of furry four feet. I decided to visit several animal shelters. I ambitiously visited three in one week. When I looked at Paws No-kill shelter, I came across two cats which grabbed my attention.

One cat, named Winston, was a silver two-year male cat who was quite friendly as he walked around sniffing people. The other cat was a 10-month old female grey-stripped Tabby named Jynx. She portrayed herself as more of an independent. With opposite opinions during discussion, the conclusion was my husband wanted Jynx, and I wanted Winston.

As I sat and watched the two cats at the shelter, Jynx tried to stick her paw on another cat's nose. She ran around the room and didn't seem to fit the average Lap Cat image, which is what I normally would choose. We left the animal haven to give it more thought.

Since my time and patience was running short for visiting more shelters, and my bleeding heart of vulnerability was wanting to adopt, I thought I would visit Paws one more time. As the volunteer escorted me to the cat room, I walked through the door hoping the two cats were still there and they were. I saw Jynx jump down from the counter where she perched to harass another cat.

The supervising lady said, "No, Jynx."

I giggled at the sight.

Jynx immediately put down her paw. She walked around and hopped into the litter box to do her duty. After seeing this, I choose Jynx. Even with all the commotion of cats wandering around, she knew how and when to use the litter box. This was the determining factor for me.

I quickly announced to the lady, "I will take Jynx."

She said, "Okay, I will get her ready. You don't have other cats at home do you?"

"No." I replied.

"Good, because she does not like other cats."

As the lady packed her up and I paid the fee, I was confident with my choice. At this point, I will let Jynx tell the story.

At the time, I was only ten months old. I remember being placed in a cardboard box with holes on top and a handle. As I peeked out one of the holes, I saw this lady with brown hair driving. I stared at her and I kept meowing. I wanted to know what she was doing. "Lady, where am I going?" The car stopped and the garage door noisily came down. The lady retrieved me from the back seat of the car in my box as she stepped inside her home and placed me on the floor.

She opened the box and reached for me to take me out. She said, "There."

As I looked around, I was afraid; then I hid at the bottom of the stairs. The lady sat calmly down in her easy chair so I jumped on her lap and nestled my face on her chin. I needed to put my scent there. I think she was my new Mom. The litter box was back at the bottom of the stairs so I went back to hide there.

Around 4:30 p.m., a man entered the door of the home. "Honey, I'm home." This man looked at me and said, "Oh, you got Jynx!" For the rest of the night I laid on my new Papa's lap. My momma said I was this man's birthday gift. I could tell he liked me as he smiled with affection.

The first few days were fine. I had my favorite food, water, a litter box and a bed with two warm bodies to sleep on. The only negative was my front claws were removed.

When Mom was outside cutting the grass, I fell asleep in the window watching her. Ideally, I found this to be a warm home.

A YEAR LATER. I heard my momma and my papa talking last night. She said a house guest would be staying with us in two weeks. I'm not sure who this would be. They seemed happy yet concerned about me.

A week later, I happen to be looking out the window. A big black four-legged animal was in our back yard. OMG! As I looked at it running around the yard sniffing, the animal dropped logs like

I normally drop in my litter pan. Was this a bear? Was this a wolf? By golly, Mom called it a DOG.

The first time our eyes met was through the sliding glass door. I arched my back and fluffed my tail like a raccoon and this bear, I mean, dog ran away in fear from my frightening dramatical sight. I knew this was going to be fun. I was curious, so curious about this dog. However, she was over 50 pounds and I am only 10. I knew I had to be careful, although I needed to show her who was boss! Our parents had us social distance for a while. They weren't sure if we would get along, but I wanted to befriend this creature.

We were supervised as we smelled each other from a distance. Our kibbles of food were different smelling, and as I sniffed her mouth, I realized this creature does personal hygiene just like me.

Every night the dog stayed in the basement, and outside during the day. I often peeked downstairs to see this creature. From the day she came home, they called her, "Ashlee."

As another week went by, Ashlee was making a, "Bark, bark," sound during the night.

As I tossed and turned in my parents' warm bed, I thought, "Let's bring her upstairs, folks, so we can all get some sleep."

The cage Ashlee stayed in was brought upstairs to the living room. As Ashlee nestled in her cage on the blanket, she was satisfied. We finally slept throughout the night.

During the day, I peeked around the corner with my slit eyes since the bright sun was shining. I saw Ashlee and she saw me; I immediately arched my back and fluffed my raccoon tail. Ashlee's brown eyes opened wide and tail stayed still. Momma pulled Ashlee's lease to guide her to the other room.

Other times while Ashlee sat in the great room, I courageously jumped from the half-wall in our kitchen to the brown couch near Ashlee. She jumped away seeing my bold act. She turned her head to see me, then laid down. I think she was getting used to my tricks.

When Ashlee ran in the house from the outside, the remnants of dark round kibbles, that I call leftover bunny caviar, fell from her mouth onto the kitchen floor.

Mama yelled, "Ashlee!"

In my heart, I understood. I said, "Meow, I like to eat flies and spiders." No human could probably relate to this I'm sure.

After two months of our shenanigans, and smelling nose to nose, I finally thought, "Well, I'm staying, and she is not going, so maybe we should be friends." At this time, I was over a year old, and Ashlee, still a puppy at two years.

FIVE YEARS LATER, "I just love Ashlee." She has four legs and a tail just like me. Her ears fold over while mine are triangular and perky. In the morning we sit side-by-side in the kitchen waiting for Papa to feed us. Ashlee just stares while I meow to be heard, "I want a treat!"

Other times, I sit perched on the counter starring, as my sister pokes momma with her cold-wet nose and starts salivating. After we finish breakfast, she stretches and I smell Ashlee's feet. When she stands, I run under her as if it was the Brooklyn Bridge.

If I am unsure of a situation with her, I just quiver my tail back and forth in uncertainty. When Ashlee acknowledges this, she tries to make me feel comfortable.

I still guard my water bowl downstairs though, when Ashlee runs upstairs and I hide around the corner, I bat, bat, bat her when she runs past me.

My reality is whatever Ashlee does, I just love and cherish her. "She will always be my Big Sister because I trust her."

Animal Axioms

by Jolee L. Price

Hearty and boisterous laughter greeted me as I walked across the patio with lunch for my grown-up twins, Katie and Jonny and me.

"What's so funny?" I asked as I set the tray down.

"We're just having some old-fashioned animal axiom fun Mom, as my dear brother would lovingly articulate, sparked by the past." Taking a grilled cheese sandwich, and facing her brother before relishing two large bites, continued, "I'm as a hungry as a horse."

"Careful Katie, the way you're chowing down, you'll soon be saying you feel like a beached whale right before you start waddling like a duck."

Laughing, she spat out her food, and snorted. "Cut it out Jonny, I'm trying to eat."

"I find it amusing after all these years that you still snort when you laugh."

Mom whispered, "Jonny, don't say snort, our neighbors are cops."

"Aw, come on Ma; the neighbors know our sister penguin here."

That comment caused a backhand to the back of my head.

"Ma! You know Katie was nicknamed the "Penguin" because she always wore black and white and looked like a nun."

"That's because I was trying to emulate our late, Great Aunt, Sister Lucy."

Simultaneously, we all made the Sign of the Cross as Mom said, "May she rest in peace."

Sitting down, Mom handed us our drinks and looking at Jonny, asked, "What brought up the axioms?"

"Memory Lane, Ma; tell her Katie."

Katie reached for her notebook. "When Jonny and I were finishing cleaning up the garage for you this morning, I noticed my old Barbie suitcase on the bottom of Dad's work bench. Do you remember when you and Dad let us go to summer camp?"

"Yes, I do. You were both twelve." Motioning to the notebook, "Is that a diary from camp?"

"Not exactly. Between the nature hikes, activities, and classes, Jonny and I made a game of comparing sayings of animals with people, and we came up with this list, many of which we heard from you and Dad.

For example, there was a set of boy triplets who were antsy. They couldn't seem to focus and were always itching to do something else before they were done with what they were doing, so we marked them on our list as having ants in their pants."

"Which is funny, because we heard through the pipeline, that one brother is now a yoga instructor with his wife, and the other two brothers teach Tai Chi. Go figure."

"It's obvious they put their bottled-up energy to good use," replied Mom. "Anyone else?"

"The camp counselors definitely were busy as a bee," answered Jonny, "and there was this one little girl who took her time in EVERYTHING. We always seemed to be either waiting on and/or for her, so she was..."

"Don't tell me," interjected Mom, "slow as a turtle."

"And that's putting it mildly. Katie, do you remember the camp counselor with the curly-red hair?"

"Yes, she oozed happiness no matter what and found positivity in every situation. One morning the power went out right before breakfast. We were going to have pancakes. While some staff members went looking for the reason for the outage, she said it was the perfect opportunity to have a campfire and roast hot dogs and marshmallows. That was a breakfast we all enjoyed. Her joy and happiness were contagious, so she was our Bluebird of Happiness.

There was also one of the cooks. He never seemed to lose his cool, even when the triplets instigated a food fight. He seemed ceaseless in patience and kindness. Nothing seemed to get under his skin. You could also go to him about anything at any time. He always had an answer and was the only one we gave two sayings to which were gentle as a lamb and wise as an owl.

There are more comparisons, but without going through every detail, here are more sayings that made our list such as memory like an elephant, cunning as a fox, soar like an eagle, and ears like a bat, to name a few."

"You two obviously had an interesting group."

"We did. Katie and I truly had a great time. With you and Pop being so protective, we were amazed at being allowed to go to camp. Axioms aside, you're definitely a mother hen and Pop watched us all like a hawk."

"True, but birds do have to leave their nests sooner or later, and summer camp was a starting lesson at being away from home."

Reaching for her hand, Katie said, "We never really leave Mom, we always come back home to roost."

"To which I am grateful and now, if you're ready for dessert, this Mother Hen has baked a cherry pie with our names on it."

Animals and Feelings

by Emilia Weindorfer

Looking at a dog or cat who has become a family member, it becomes apparent that a bond exists with that pet that is mutually satisfying. There is a look of contentment on the pet's face when eye contact is made.

Dogs communicate to their owners with their eyes, just as humans do with them. Their eyes tell us many of the feelings they have when we make eye contact. Their eyes are truly a window to their souls just as ours are to us. Along with their eyes, their mouths signify emotion too.

Some dogs appear happy most of the time you are with them, as if their mouths are smiling. The tail may be wagging too. Tails are a good barometer of feelings along with the eyes.

Other animals like birds also communicate with their eyes. When our pet albino cockatiel Chico was alive, he demonstrated his affection for us by showing us dreamy eyes when you spoke to him. He also responded with happy, high-pitched chirps.

Animals in the wild demonstrate similar behaviors. They bond with their parents learning how to survive from their mothers. She teaches them to search safely for food, how to sense danger and stay away from it, build or seek shelter, and bond with their peers to eventually mate to continue the species.

Patron saint of animals and ecologist, St. Francis of Assisi, devoted his life to animals, addressed sermons to birds, and domesticate wolves. Wolves spend their lives in hierarchal groups called packs, exchange information about dominance and territory through scent, sound, and body language. Beavers and prairie dogs cooperate with others of their kind in building and excavating, and by warning each other of danger. Whales and porpoises communicate with their species through a complex system of squeaks, trills and bellows.

River otters are gregarious and fun-loving animals that seem to spend as much time romping and paying as they do hunting and fishing. Not even a deep covering of snow will deter them from sliding down riverbanks and plunging into icy water. This sociable family group is often joined by others to toboggan in the snow down muddy river banks or frolic occasionally in the water talking to each other with a varied repertoire of growls, chirps and squeals.

Dr. Jane Goodall was a tireless worker in Tanzania's Gombe preserve. She observed a chimpanzee she later named David Greybeard, doing object modification-picking up a small, leafy twig and stripping it of its leaves to use as a tool for digging.

She discovered that many of the wild chimpanzees' postures and gestures-kissing, embracing, holding hands, patting one another on the back, swaggering, punching, kicking, pinching, tickling, somersaulting, and pirouetting are common to human culture and in the same context as for us. They displayed long term affection and supportive bonds between family members and close friends. They helped and cared for each other. They could bear grudges lasting more than a week. They wandered about in small groups like so any of our teens.

79

The similarities between animals and humans are totally amazing.

Fluffy

by Jane Binner

My early childhood was a blur of outdoor adventures in my rural neighborhood, on the outskirts of a small and developing town in northeastern Illinois, still transitioning from farmland to community. Any season, my younger brother and I were outside more than in. I was a tomboy. Girls bored me, with their Barbie townhouses and polite play. I captured banana spiders and crayfish and garden snakes. I rescued fallen birds. I hung with the neighborhood boys often, even more than my brother did, running through cornfields, building forts (even a snow fort in the blizzard of '79), playing football and baseball in our half-acre empty lot. Ghosts in the Graveyard on summer nights. Each and every summer I ran barefoot until the first bee sting.

Our family had a pet dog, Sam – a white beagle with black spots and a good temperament – and I had my cat, Fluffy. He was a tomcat who roamed the neighborhood every day as I did. I imagine he went to the nearby farm and sought out mice. I know he must have also gotten into fights as he was plagued with injuries. There always seemed to be fresh blood matting his fur when he returned at night. There was also that ever-present scrape on his hind leg that never quite healed. He and I explored and adventured during the day – separately – and came in at night and slept – exhausted.

In those early years, my father seemed to work steadily only in the summers as a union carpenter and was laid off most every winter. We were rather poor, and I wore clothes from garage sales more than I ever wore something new. When my father drifted in on summer nights, exhausted from work, or on winter afternoons after unsuccessfully looking for work - just in time for dinner and the evening news before retiring for the night – experience told us it best to just let him be.

Our mother was available. She was the constant. Always in the kitchen, with Paul Harvey on the radio. She was also a hovering and stifling presence in our lives. All our neighborhood friends had more relaxed and uninvolved mothers. Their toys got to lay about their yards. Their moms didn't check up on them throughout the day. Their moms did not pay sitters for one and two-hour stints, but rather our friends' parents left and let them run amok. Our mother infuriated us, and yet I admit now, looking back, there was also a comfort in the continuity of it. The daily routine. Dinner at five. Forced to eat what she cooked, or we didn't eat. There was a soothing quality to our routine, and little actual conflict. We would argue curfews and bedtimes, but little else worthy of note. No day is vivid in my memory, differing from any other, until the summer I was eight.

"I HATE YOU!" I screamed as I slammed my door. My mom got rid of Fluffy. She GOT RID OF my cat. How could she? What did Fluffy ever do? My mom said he had peed on the couch. This was the first I was hearing of this. Fluffy was a tomcat and outside during the day. He slept with me in my room every night. When did he have the occasion to pee in the living room?

I wouldn't speak to my mother for weeks. I came out only to eat. I cried every single day, all day. Finally, when it became apparent I would not forgive her, my mom made a peace offering in the form of an 18-pound black cat named Domino. Oh, how I hated that replacement cat! The only animal I ever hated, and through no fault of his own. My mother's very act of getting another cat only distanced me further from her. The act was proof she had no consideration for my feelings, thinking any cat would do. I would never really trust her again.

After that summer, I withdrew, and part of my routine became time alone as well. Climbing the Weeping Willow in our backyard, always a notebook and pen in my pocket, jotting down my thoughts and poems. Writing became my refuge. At some point, I stopped searching out Fluffy and his injured leg in every orange tabby I came across. (I always imagined some grand escape from the shelter for him.) When I reached junior high, I stopped climbing that tree, but rather I would walk up to the weigh station and watch the cars on I-80 pass. I spent endless summer and fall evenings there well into high school.

Sometimes even now, my mom tells the story of Fluffy. She changes the details. The reasons why she did it. I don't think she knows what the truth is anymore. I think it's her way of trying to find a way in, acknowledging the damage done by that one act, without apologizing or admitting wrong. I have seen it all with new eyes as well. I am glad I didn't see it sooner. It kept the illusion in place longer. It seemed like an isolated incident at the time. I have my own kids now, and I've done wrong by them. I see that it's not in the actual betrayal where the unforgivable pain lies, as much as in the dispelling of the myth of a happy childhood. The proceeding through life without an anchor anymore. The entrance of uncertainty in life where none had existed before.

When I reflect on my failed relationship with both my parents, I always linger on that one day. My father responding "ask your mother" when I ask if he had seen Fluffy. He wouldn't look at me and I think I knew then that something was wrong. I remember walking down those dozen or so steps to the basement where my mother was putting laundry through her wringer washer. She told me what she had done as casually as though she was reciting what unpalatable meal she would be serving for dinner. At the time, it could almost have seemed trivial – a childhood trauma built to monumental levels in an immature mind. However, it is the one event in childhood, which is evidence that those tendencies were there even then. Those tendencies that have become more readily apparent to me now in recent years. My mother's cold and erratic nature. My father's passivity.

As the years passed, things would change. The boys noticed I was a girl, and no longer wanted to just play with me. The man down the street ran oil into his ditch one summer so we would stop hanging around looking for crayfish in the creek near his backyard. My Weeping Willow was struck by lightning one spring and split in half. I even stopped going to the weigh station after a rather scary incident with a truck driver. All my refuges evaporated one by one. As did my trust in the people closest to me. Sometimes I wonder if I could take away that one day, whether everything would have turned out differently for me. A child's perception of one event, forever tugging at my happiness.

Creek Bed Birth

by Awesome Angie Engstrom

"Baby Cow! Are you drowning?"

Did anyone see?

Creek bed birth! She's struggling for life.

Baby Cow needs my help and I'm stuck in this school bus for five more miles. I saw her. I looked right into Mama Cow's yearning eyes. Her newborn calf is stuck in the muck and mud of Silver Creek.

"Get up, Baby Cow. Before you drown!"

The entire herd of dairy cows locked eyes on me through the school bus window as I sped by, as if they were all pleading for my help. This is the scene that just flashed before me from the school bus window as we sped by the Klenke Farm. I shot up with perfect posture, inhaled deep, and held my breath. My 10-year-old heart and mind are racing. Inside my heart I yelled, "Baby Cow is drowning! Did anyone else just see that?"

Desperately looking around the bus, I hoped to see that someone else noticed too. Everyone is in their own, little, numbed out school bus mode. No one seemed to notice. All I saw was a boy about my age staring out the window on the opposite side of the bus. A little girl playing with her dolls. An older girl reading a Little House on the Prairie book. And a few other kids that obviously had not seen what I saw.

Baby Cow is drowning! And I am the only one who noticed. I knew in my gut I had to speak up, but would anyone listen?

Joey's a safe bus driver.

I know she cares -- but

Baby Cow is not her priority.

As much time as I spend on this school bus, you'd think I'd know the kids better; but I don't. Joey, our bus driver -- bless her heart -- she does her job well, always demanding quieter, inside voices as she focuses on driving the narrow, hilly country roads. It seems like any time I talk, she makes me sit in the dreaded, lonely front seat. Unfortunately, I have not mastered volume control, so it's become easier to say nothing than to try talking to anyone on the bus. I learned from experience that any time I open my mouth, my voice is loud and full of energy and not welcome on the school bus... or in the classroom... or at home.

Wow – no wonder I never feel heard.

I learned that sharing my voice and the true, spirited Me are not welcome in my world. Keeping my thoughts and perspectives to myself has become my safe place. Therefore, I do not feel safe talking with Joey. And I don't know any of the other passengers well enough to share what I just saw.

I am certain Joey didn't see because she was focused on her driving. From high up in the bus, my view looking out the passenger window and over the edge, into the valley was perfect for me to see down into the creek bed below the road level. Any driver could not see the scene that I saw.

Baby Cow is not safe, and I am certain I am the only living being who noticed. The anxiety vacuumed me into a hyper-focused, alert state with one goal – to save Baby Cow.

I'm scared for Baby Cow's life.

This stupid bus route!

Time travel needs to be a thing.

Ugh! This goofed up bus route! Joey, you just passed my house. I can see it from my window, a quarter mile across the field. No, I can't get off yet. I have to ride the five-mile loop into three other neighborhoods before they turn down my street to let me off. Why does this route have to take so long? You are wasting my time, stupid Bus Route.

In my neighborhood, each house is about a mile from the next, separated by open farmland. When the crops are low to the ground, I can see for miles. And sitting high up in the school bus, I have an even better view. The bus route still has fifteen more minutes of winding through country roads to get to my drop off. More time than I need to plan my rescue mission – and not panic. I know I have to get home fast and let Dad know so he can call the Klenke farm, but I have to wait it out.

Lord, please keep Baby Cow safe until I can get her help.

The way the roads were laid out, I understood why the route was designed as it was. It's annoying, but at some point I accepted the reality of it and learned how to numb out. But today – the wait was agonizing! Baby Cow's life was in danger.

I'm just a 10-year-old girl

From my experience,

I'm not worthy of respect.

Dad will be home, so I will go directly to him and tell him what I saw. He will know what to do. Adults always know what to do. But will he listen to me? Will he take me seriously? I'm just a 10-year-old girl that from my perspective, does not get much respect. It seems that no one listens to me. I have thoroughly convinced myself that my thoughts and opinions do not matter.

I am not timid or shy. Quite the opposite. Loud and full of energy. But to some people in the world loud and full of energy translates to disruptive and annoying.

"Quiet down. Why do you have to be so loud?" These were phases I heard quite often.

Baby Cow is worth being loud today. I just have to wait until it's safe for me to speak up.

Act as if it's up to me

To prove that love exists.

My voice can save a life.

Baby Cow's safety trumped my fear. I did speak up. Dad made the phone call. And Mr. Klenke is extremely grateful.

My voice saved Baby Cow today.

This experience proved to me that everyone and everything has meaning and purpose… including bus routes.

"Your voice saved my life. Thank You."

Love, Baby Cow

The Beast

by Kathleen C. Z. Klevorn

Was that a growl that I just heard? As I was running down the path, trees and shadows lined the trail. Something was not right and I could feel it in my bones. I started breathing heavily, slowing down and listening to my body. My heart was racing and I felt faint. What was going on? I never dreamed that I was being stalked. A few weeks later, I learned the beast stalking me was cancer.

It's hard to describe the feelings one has when given the diagnosis of cancer. Mine were a jumble of shock, disbelief, fear, anger, and despair. What was multiple myeloma? Where would I go for treatment? How would I be able to survive? The questions kept coming and I had very few answers.

The doctors told me not to read too much on the internet because a lot of the information was not current, but I couldn't help myself. I did some research, learned more about the disease and was shocked again by the poor prognosis. Most gave survival rates in months not years. For me, this was not acceptable. Let the battle begin!

I was referred to a multiple myeloma specialist who was conducting a clinical trial at the University of Chicago. Perfect timing! My husband and I talked with the study team there and decided this was the best course of treatment for me. We would attack this beast with the latest treatment available. Most specialists agreed that this would be the best hope for a long remission.

The months of treatment were difficult. I had eighteen cycles of a three-drug regimen and an autologous stem cell transplant that required seventeen days of hospitalization in an isolation unit. My body was poked and prodded and driven to the depths of existence both physically and mentally While I was alone in my hospital room, it gave me a lot of time to reflect and try to tame the beast within me using prayer, meditation and journaling. Throughout the ordeal, I turned to the three stalwarts in my life for help: faith, family and friends. Without their support, I truly believe that I would not be here today. There is definitely an emotional and mental component to healing.

I started each day with prayer to give me strength. My husband, Joe, was my caregiver and spent many nights at the hospital even though I was out of it a lot of the time. He was there to keep me company when I was coherent. When he wasn't there and I was feeling lonely, a friend would call or a family member would visit. One group of friends shared their pictures wearing hats, because I lost my hair and would be wearing hats for a while. They let me know that even though I was physically in isolation, I was not alone. When I was packing up to go home from the hospital, I was feeling a little anxious and wondering if I was ready. Then, I found a brown rosary on the floor with two medals, unlike any I had ever seen before. I asked the nurses and all of my friends who had visited and it didn't belong to any of them. Since I was in isolation, I don't know how the rosary got in my room. When I looked closer, one of the medals was of Padre Pio. His words inspired me and assured me that I was ready to go home.

"Let us face the present trials to which divine providence subjects us, but let us not lose heart or become discouraged. Let us fight valiantly, and we will obtain the prize of strong souls. Remember the words the divine Master spoke one day to the Apostles and which he says to you today, 'Do not let your hearts be troubled.' Yes, let not your heart be troubled in the hour of trial because Jesus promised his real assistance to those who follow him."

-Padre Pio

I know the beast is still lurking and could strike again at any time. When I hear the grumble begin, I turn again to my support system, the big three: faith, family and friends. I know they are there for me and it brings me peace and confidence that I can call on them for whatever I need to get through the challenges ahead.

It has been almost six years since I ran down that path and knew that something was wrong. I am filled with gratitude every single day that I get out of bed to continue this fight. I do what I can to defeat the beast that is multiple myeloma for me, and cancer for so many others. This has become one of my passions in life. It gives me purpose. I hope someday we can say the beast that is cancer has been defeated and we have found a cure. Until then I continue to hope that all we are doing in this fight ultimately leads to a cure. Together, let's slay the beast!

Don't Be Nosey

by Diane Perry

One day Mom called me. "Hey, do you want to go to the zoo with your sisters and their families?"

I answered, "Sure, I would love to go."

When Saturday approached, all of us drove to the Brookfield Zoo. We got there promptly at 10:00 a.m. when it opened. The zoological park covers an area of 216 acres and has 2300 animals of different species.

After we viewed the reptile house, the giraffes, elephants, and the zebras, we decided to ride the tram to the west side of the park to visit the farm petting zoo. It was a balmy day.

As my nieces followed their parents into the exhibit, we first visited the cows, horses and the pigs. A relaxed pig was wallowing in the mud.

The kids remarked, "He is all dirty."

Mom said, "He is trying to keep cool."

A nearby pond nestled ducks of different species and their ducklings. We peeked in at the chicken coop and bought a handful of feed to give them through the fence. It felt funny as the chickens pecked in our hands.

My niece, Stacy said, "Let's go see the goats."

Her father said, "Okay, let's go," being the first to lead the way.

As all of us entered the gates of the petting zoo, as the baby goats, one named Rhubarb and the other named Ginger ran exuberantly to us. A big brown goat weighing over one hundred pounds jumped on the bench next to where Mom was sitting. Mom, being a diabetic, kept treats like crackers, raisins or cheese in her purse.

The curious goat pushed his nose in Mom's lap and further to open her purse to smell the treats.

All of a sudden, Mom grabbed her treasured treat bag defensively and slammed the goat over his head. Wham! "Get outta here!" She snapped quickly.

Stunned, the goat gave Mom a surprised look. He turned his head from side to side with a deep look of thought on his face.

As we all panicked, I ran to the puzzled goat and patted him on the head saying, "Nice goat, it's okay, it's okay."

The goat hopped off the bench quickly and proceeded to the other side of the petting area where children holding treats seemed more friendly.

Upon exiting the petting zoo safely, we all roared with laughter as to this quick draw on the part of my mother.

Mom said, "When are we having lunch?"

My sister, Gayle said, "How about twelve o'clock?"

Everyone agreed to the time. Even though I was hungry, I didn't dare to help myself to the treasured treat bag.

Bunyan's Babe

by Jolee L. Price

Slamming the front door behind me causing a ripple effect of an echo throughout our newly purchased home for refurbishing and reselling, loudly announced my arrival. My fiancé runs into the foyer, and before he can utter one word, I defiantly say, "That's it; that's it; that's it! I am keeping my maiden name when we marry and no, I will not even dignify your last name with a hyphen."

The words "here we go again" come to mind. Knowing the cause for her outburst, I still ask, "Honey, what's wrong?"

"You know what's wrong! Your family needs to get some group counseling going on with their folklore obsession; especially your brother."

"Did Joe rile you up again?"

Sighing, my shrugged and stooped shoulders answered his question.

Reaching out to hug me, "Babe, don't be blue."

Immediately stepping back, "Blue? Really? You and your brother are two peas in a pod, Paul. The comments and gestures never stop."

"Sorry. What did Joe do or say this time?"

"He had a caricature of us made with your face on the body of a muscular lumberjack and my face on the body of a blue ox. We're standing next to each other and written on top is "Love is

Grand" followed by a dash and then "Our Family Traditions Continue," and it's hanging on THE wall inside his diner. Joe told me we now have a place of honor with all the other caricatures."

"He's got a point. Those caricatures are Joe's way of getting to know his customers, regulars and visitors alike."

"You're not helping."

"You know my dad's boyhood heroes are Paul Bunyan and his faithful sidekick, Babe the Blue Ox. Gramps was the one who got him started on them by telling him stories of Bunyan as a logger with tremendous physical strength along with a skill set no other logger had and his companion who happened to be a blue ox whose frolics paralleled those of a dog. My dad was so fascinated by a blue ox that he wanted his very own, but since he couldn't, every dog he's had has been named Babe. You've had the great pleasure of meeting Babe VII.

I remember for Dad's 50th birthday, Mom gave him a Blue German Shepherd. There was just something extra special about that dog and was the only one he had that he named Sir Babe.

Come to think of it, Dad still has a 1916 promotional pamphlet for the Red River Lumber Company that Gramps gave him written by freelancer William B. Laughead. He not only popularized Bunyan, but later took many liberties with the original oral source material he received, like noting that Bunyan and Babe are said to have created the 10,000 Lakes of Minnesota by their footprints while other authors credited Bunyan with creating the Grand Canyon by pulling his ax behind him and Mount Hood by putting stones on his campfire."

"Thanks for the umpteenth rerun history lesson, but it doesn't change the fact that your family gets carried away."

"Hey, my dad says it started with Gramps, but my mom told me that once my dad held me in his arms after I was born, she could tell by his grin what he wanted to name me, and here I am, Paul Bunyan, about to marry the love of my life, who just happens to be named Babe; talk about fate. Never in my wildest dreams, did I even speculate meeting a woman named Babe."

"To this day, I still don't know how or why my parents came up with my name."

"I'm glad they did. I remember the day I told my family I met "the one" they were happy for me, but when I told them your name, they were ecstatic. There were almost visible flashes of light in the room by the light bulbs going off in their heads."

"Aren't we the lucky ones."

"We are, Babe. Just think of the fun and memories we created. We've been to Bangor, Maine, which claims to be both the birthplace of the lumber industry and the birthplace of Bunyan. We've been to Bemidji, Minnesota, which claims to be the home of Bunyan and Babe, and don't forget your favorite trip to the Trees of Mystery near Klamath, California. You not only loved the trees, but you really got into the sculptures and carvings illustrating the stories of Bunyan and his crew."

"Those trips were memories in the making and hopefully, God-willing, we'll have many more."

"Look, I can ask my family to cut you some slack. I'll even ask Joe to take our caricature off the wall."

"No, don't do that. Truth be told, I've always enjoyed and appreciated the camaraderie of your family and how everyone gets into Paul Bunyan and his blue ox, Babe. Your family knows how to have a lot of fun and because of them and you, I have too. You've all shown me what it's like to enjoy life and not just exist."

"Then what's going on? Are our wedding plans along with the rehabbing of this log cabin too much right now?"

"Life has been a bit overwhelming lately." Taking a deep breath and looking over the room, a grin forms into a Cheshire cat smile.

"I see the flash of a light bulb going off."

"Indeed, you do. I can't believe I didn't realize this before. I'm just now finding it amusing that our latest real estate investment happens to be a log cabin home. I think this proves fate is at work once again. I believe this is our home Mr. Bunyan. After all, it falls in the line of family tradition."

"I couldn't agree more." Leaning in to kiss her, she pauses and looks up into his eyes.

"But I swear, if your brother's toast for us at our wedding reception includes the newly married couple being a lumberjack and his ox, I'll deck him."

What the Cluck?

by Paula Morris Thomas

Oh my God! There's another one! They're everywhere! What the cluck!

Phewwwww. Let me hide out here and catch my breath for a minute.

I was lucky to come upon this overturned half-barrel planter with the two missing slats. The opening is snug but it was big enough for me to wriggle through to have a place to hide and write out my last will and testament.

I know that I'm gonna be a goner soon if it's true that history repeats itself. Let me explain to you.

My name is Hannah Hen. I'm the third Hannah...sharing the name with my mother and grandmother. And I remember the stories that grandma used to tell me that her daddy used to tell her.

See...when great-grandpa Randy Rooster was a little cockerel, his daddy, great-great grandpa Rufus Rooster, who was known as Papa Rufus, told him stories about the man who lived up the block that came up with this great new recipe and technique for frying chicken.

He got great reviews from people near and far. And he was such a kind gentleman that everybody and everything loved him...unless you was a chicken.

He was constantly working on fine tuning and perfecting the recipe...and to do that, what do you think he needed? That's right! Chickens.

Papa Rufus told stories about the chickens that didn't come home at the end of their day of struttin' and scratchin' around the many barnyards in the area. Nobody could figure it out at first. Didn't know if they were running away from home on purpose or meeting some untimely end by straying too far from home accidentally.

Then one day some of the older roosters and hens were talking under the big oak tree on the Myers family's property. A few of them mentioned that it seemed like fowl started disappearing when you would see the fried chicken man in that white suit with blood spatters, and his string necktie, and that little hatchet in his hand...and a mask on his face.

They understood the white suit and the string tie 'cause they had seen his likeness on posters nailed to enough trees and fence posts, and plastered on the side of his car and some of the cabs that brought people home from shopping uptown. But they couldn't understand the mask...until the one day when Rooster Greg Gotaway told all the other survivors what he'd heard before he escaped.

Fried Chicken Man was talking to his son, Fried Chicken Boy, and giving him some pointers about the fried chicken business.

He said, "Son, you gotta know why I wear what I wear."

"I wear the white suit because it makes me look warm...friendly... trustworthy. The string tie makes me look like a gentleman. The mask has two purposes. One...it hides my fake smile which is really a sneer. And two...you don't breathe in any deadly germs that can get in your nostrils when you chop the heads off and gut the chickens."

"All they see are my kind eyes. And if I don't put on a mask then know that I'm going out to take care of business."

All the roosters and chickens clucked and nodded in delight for this heads up gift of insight. They created squawk and cluck signals to use to identify if Fried Chicken Man exited his house with or without a mask.

Maskless meant safety and was signaled by three calm clucks. Masked meant head to the hills and hide and was signaled by a rapid succession of a dozen clucks.

So now I'm here, remembering them stories, thankful for this half-barrel temporary hiding place, wondering how much time do I have before I end up in the fryer.

I'm seeing masked faces everywhere!

What the cluck!

That can't be a good sign for a chicken anywhere! We are severely outnumbered!

But you know what... now that I think about it...nobody has really chased after me...and I don't see any hatchets in anybody's hand... and the eyes above the masks look more worried and frightened than kind.

What the cluck is going on?

Note from the author -- I thought of the joke "why did the chicken cross the road?... to get away from Colonel Sanders" and this little story was birthed.

Please know that I am not taking lightly the fatal effect that this COVID-19 corona virus pandemic is having in our country and around the world. I am sorrowful for those who have lost their lives to this challenging disease...and I am praying for their surviving family members, friends, and loved ones who are affected by the passings.

Importance

by Dawn E. Plestina

One moonlit evening, in a community not so far away, lived animals who could not agree with each other and constantly argued about who was the most important.

Bear proclaimed louder than the crashing waves, "We, the land animals of this world, dominate with our strength."

Spraying Bear with water from its blowhole, Whale bellowed, "We, the sea animals of this world, are older than you. We dominate with our experience."

Located between these two mighty beasts and zigzagging on the beach between the sea and the land, Salamander grabbed their attention with, "We, the amphibians, are the best; we dominate because we understand both your land and sea habitats."

Simultaneously, Bear and Whale roared with laughter.

"You have no idea what you are," started Bear.

"...because you can't choose!" chimed Whale.

And simultaneously they finished with "so there is no way your kind dominates anything!"

Above the din circled Owl who screeched, "Enough! Boasting does not strengthen you, and diminishing others only demonstrates that you are compensating for your weaknesses. Each of your groups has importance; you do not need to dominate one another. Put your energy into continually cooperating because that can help you all collectively. You can all benefit, and you can all win."

Taken aback, Bear, Whale, and Salamander stared at Owl, then at one another. Salamander proposed a plan for the land, sea, and amphibian communities. "Bear, you see many humans litter the beaches with items that kill sea life. Will and your fellow land animals watch for those who litter and ensure they pick up after themselves?"

"I can round up my most fierce friends and monitor the beach, but what will the sea life do to help us?" queried Bear.

"Whale, can you gather your most intimidating sea creatures to keep ships as far away from shore as possible? Often times hunters disembark to hunt the land animals for their fur and other trophy-like wants.

Whale answered with "I guarantee the creatures of the sea will put a stop to this human intervention."

Thusly, Bear and the land animals used their strength to ensure the humans threw their garbage away or recycled it in appropriate containers. Whale and the sea animals devised clever blockades which kept the hunters from killing land animals. Salamander and the rest of the amphibians kept the lines of communication open between the land and sea life. And Owl looked over them all with pride.

Moral: Every group has importance and working together brings strength to all.

We Were Friends

by Sylvester Kapocius

Over the years I became familiar with some of the animals' habits and behavior. They are smart. I saw how nature provided them with a gift. Their extraordinary sense of security, and self-preservation, some of which I lack.

One time my dog Tipper provided that to me. I tried to feed him some cheese that contained some chemical preservatives. It required no refrigeration. He took a whiff of it and walked away without eating it. I knew he was hungry. Then I placed the same brand of cheese with no preservatives in it before him. He smelled it then gobbled it up in a few seconds.

I bought him a tick-free collar that was labeled irradiated. I threw it on the floor in the clothes closet. I waited until he showed me it was time for him to do his duty outdoors. I shouted to him, "Tipper, go get your collar."

It was the first time he used his new collar.

He always got excited when I shouted that order. This time it was different. When he put his nose to it, he walked back to me without it and an apologetic look that said to me, "I don't want that collar on me."

I suspected that the fleas would not cling to Tipper if that collar was on him.

How is it that the dog and the fleas sense the danger of radiation, but we humans cannot?

Radiation cannot be seen, felt, heard, smelled, or tasted.

When I first moved to Missouri as a permanent resident, the weeds were high around the house.

One morning after breakfast, Betty and I had coffee outside on the patio. We enjoyed the cool breeze off the lake. In the quiet atmosphere, we could only hear the small waves hitting the shoreline.

I turned my head and saw a tiny creature peeking at us from out of the bushes. It was a ground squirrel. Some people call them chipmunks. It was so cute.

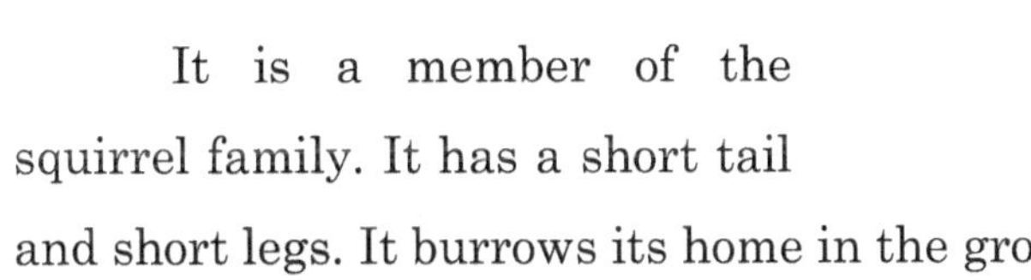

It is a member of the squirrel family. It has a short tail and short legs. It burrows its home in the ground.

This particular one studied us for at least 10 minutes. Then he finally approached us, step-by-step with caution. At first I feared it could be ratted. I am paranoid when it comes to dealing with wild animals.

I was shocked by its next move. It leapt from the ground onto the table where we sat. Then it jumped on my shoulder and attempted to grab the cookie I held in my hand. That scared the heck out of me. I felt he forced his friendship on me.

Right then, I found a way for him to earn a cookie.

I placed a long, one-inch-wide stick at a steep angle against the second-floor porch railing. His cookie was up there. He zipped up there quickly, got it, ate it, and came down by me for another one. The next day he was back for more, but I had no more.

I had fun playing with that little rascal. He used our yard for his playground. He was not shy at all. Some of his kind came to play with him.

Late in the summer, the black walnut tree near our house produced a large crop of walnuts. I hit the high branches with a long pole and more fell to the ground. I picked up over 800 that year. I soaked them, a bucket-full at a time, in a tub of water. After a day or so, I scooped them out of the water with my hands, shucked them, and laid them on a board in the sun to dry. My hands stayed brown for three days and smelled like iodine.

Days later, a few more walnuts fell off the tree to the ground. My little friend, the ground squirrel, gathered them and began burying them right next to some of the six small plants that grew along the seawall. I enjoyed watching him do that. Then a mischievous thought entered my mind. When he left, I hurriedly scooped up his buried walnuts and put them on the ground beneath the walnut tree. Then I waited for his return.

After an hour he reappeared and went straight to the walnut tree. He picked up one walnut at a time and reburied the eight walnuts back into the same exact spot he dug in the ground before. He must have seen me scoop up his buried walnuts. I would not take away his stored food he put away for the winter.

When I told Betty what I did while she was cleaning house, she yelled some nasty words at me.

The raccoon

The raccoon was another one of my pets. He liked me so well he visited me in daylight hours. I gave him a bad time, but he always came back to visit me. The first time we met was in the dark of night. It was about 2 AM. I was still in the process of building the house on the lake. We camped in a tent on the purchased lot. Me, my wife Betty, and my son Keith were still building the house.

It was very humid one night so we stayed up late. It was too warm in the tent and we had no electricity for a fan. We sat on folding chairs next to the campfire and listened to the crackling fire wood as it burned with gentle, glowing flames.

Then I heard a noise from the tree in the absolute quiet of the night. I focused my flashlight on it. I saw a raccoon sitting on a branch of the tree. He was spying on us. As I watched him, he cracked branches and threw them on the ground. He knew he got our attention, so he threw more on the ground. "What a show off," I thought.

Keith yelled out to me, "Let's play a game with them. We will find out how smart he is. Let's use the clothesline between the two trees. Tie a hotdog in the center hanging down from it."

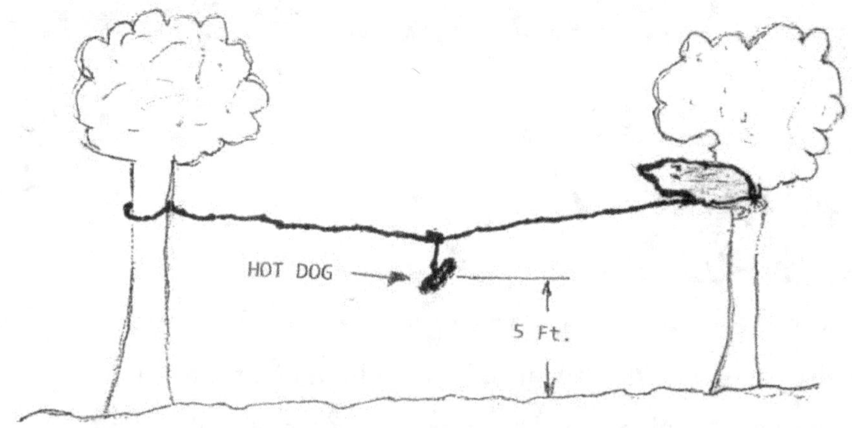

After setting the stage, we remained quiet with only whispers to each other. Soon the raccoon showed up and ran to one tree. He climbed the tree, checked the clothesline and saw he could not walk it. He climbed down and ran up the other tree and saw that it was also useless. He disappeared for a a while. When he came back, he attempted to reach the hot dog from the ground as he desperately stretched on his hind legs to reach it, but to no avail.

Keith said to me, "We won. He lost."

Most of the house was built. When winter arrived, we stayed inside the house like caterpillars in cocoons. The daily chores had to be attended to. We would clean the ashes from the log burner, bring in firewood, carry garbage to the steel drum in the cove and burn it, and once and a while visit friends up the road. At night it was always TV time. Only three channels had good reception.

One night the phone rang. It was Keith, my son, calling from Streamwood, Illinois, 500 miles away. He asked to visit with his wife and two boys. As soon as I okayed them to visit, I thought of a plan for them to meet my raccoon friend. I am sure they would get a kick out of it.

It was quite cold that night. I set my cage right outside the patio door so we could all see the raccoon get trapped in the cage.

Keith and his family finally arrived. We ate, we talked, and relaxed in the living room and watch, looking through the glass door for the raccoon to appear.

At first a strange noise was heard, like a stone rolling down the hill. My raccoon friend came up to the door looking for food. He saw some in the cage. He walked right in and as soon as he grabbed the meaty bone inside, the stick tied to the door slammed shut and he was trapped.

What he did amazed us all.

He scanned the inside of the cage with the bone still in his mouth. Then he ran from one end of the cage and struck the other and with his full body weight in an 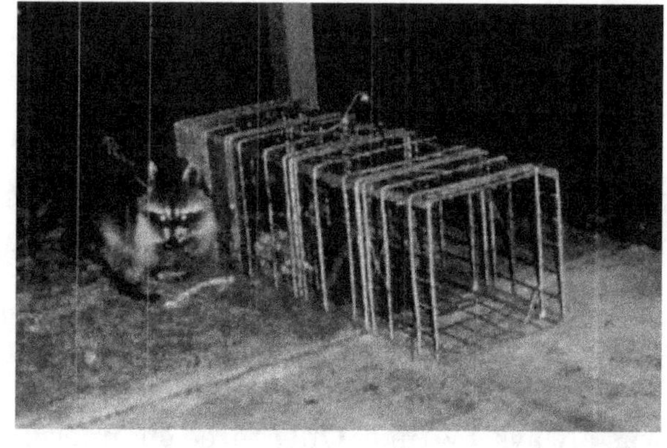 attempt to get the door open. The cage tipped slightly. He repeated his attempts to turn the cage over to get out. After three very hard bumps to the cage, it turned over, the door flopped open, and he got out. Then he mocked me as he sat beside the cage and me, being the winner.

My cage trapped another night prowler looking for food. It was the slow-moving animal in the rodent family. It was a possum.

One morning, right after breakfast, I walked outside and right to the cage. Inside was a possum sound asleep and the food was gone. I opened the door to let it out. It did not budge, like saying, "Leave me alone." I tipped the cage to drop him out. He gripped the cage and would not leave, so I left him in the cage with the door open and I walked back into the house. When I came out later he was gone.

I also had other animal friends in my life. They were all gentle. One which was owned by a relative was a German shepherd named King.

When my son, Jim, was small, he was King's best buddy. Jimmy weighed 45 pounds, and King was about 90 pounds. Whenever they wrestled together, King let him win each time, no matter how much he was abused. Both of their emotions were obvious; true friendship.

Foxy was also my friend but I never petted her, even though she might have let me.

This is how we first met. I was leery and so was she. She judged me and I judged her. I just knew we would be friends. When I came out of the house, she came out of the woods. If I wanted to see her, I whistled very loudly, once, and she appeared in a few minutes.

She lay on the grass and watched me fish on the dock. Her delight was fish, so I rewarded her with some each time I caught some for being my friend. She gripped them with her teeth and ran off into the woods to feed her five pots.

Foxy was often seen resting on the grass in front of our house.

One day after lunch, I began a walk on the gravel road up to a large hill next to our subdivision. All of the sudden, Foxy popped out of the woods and followed me on the road. Every so often I turned to see if Foxy kept pace with me. As I got to the wide bend of the road, she stopped and stared toward the woods. She faced a scrambled, stony, weeded hillside as if to tell me something. Across the ravine, out of the stony hillside, one by one her pups appeared. They sense their mother nearby. I was sure it was only for me to see her family of five pups.

Foxy was a good hunter. On two separate occasions I saw her in action. She chased ground squirrels. She would pounce on one with all of her weight, grip it with her teeth, and bring it into the woods to feed her family.

During some cold winter nights, she appeared at our door when it was difficult to find food. Being a good hunter, her visits were not often.

She was frequently seen looking down our gravel road and listening for the sound of our vehicle returning home each time. After unloading groceries, she got an apple.

When folks came out to their lake homes on weekends and holidays, Foxy and her family were not seen anywhere until they left.

There was one animal that was not too friendly, and that bothered Jimmy. It was at a large animal park we visited, located in the southeastern part of Missouri. This one animal did not let go of Jim until he got fed.

The smartest dog I had ever known

Her name was Shelby. She responded to her name instantly when called. Her eyesight, hearing, and reactions were the best I had known of any dog.

I have been told by many that to purchase a pet from some pet agency would be a gamble. What would he or she be like after taking it home?

Well, my neighbors, Brandon and Ann, don't gamble, but they got a winner. She was small when they got her. At the age of six years, she weighed about 40 pounds, and all muscle.

She is a pitbull that came from an Ibizan breed. Her brisk, attentive manner showed her intelligence. When she played she fully participated with her energy.

Ann had no fence around her yard. Shelby was trained properly and knew her boundaries, obeying her commands promptly. When she is let outside and sees me or Betty, she barks three times to be recognized. When Ann says, "Go by Lenny," she goes right over to me, and goes to others she recognizes by name.

When Betty treats her with a cracker, she jumps up and tries to kiss her.

Shelby always seemed happy and she was loyal to her keepers.

In Shelby's eyes it showed her curiosity about folks wearing masks on their faces. This is the year of the coronavirus disease. And, being a nurse, and being so dear to her dog, was prepared with masks for her family and Shelby also.

Wally Watchdog

by Paula Morris Thomas

Hi. My name is Wally...Wally watchdog. The kids thought that was a great name for the family pet...especially since that was the reason for me being purchased...to watch out for and protect the family.

And I'm sitting here on my "favoritest" perch in the whole house... the low bay window that overlooks the entire front yard, partial views of both side yards, the neighbors across the street, the letter carriers, the garbage trucks driven by the refuse engineers, the ice cream trucks in the summer, snow plows in the winter, and all the kids, and all the other furry and feathery family members.

Yeah...you'll find me looking...watching...'cause that's what watchdogs do.

I've watched the grownup people I "own" grow more and more in love with each other. And I've watched the children grow through the stages from being bratty to being beautifully behaved.

The neighborhood can also be described as a link of love. No conflict or dissension respectively and collectively. Even the furry family members get along from house to house.

From my perch I've watched and listened to the neighborhood living outside as they enjoy many block barbecues, potlucks, and picnics. Also the laughter of the kids riding their bikes and skateboards and the many impromptu basketball, baseball, and football games... followed by the skinned knees, broken arms, sprained ankles, and chipped teeth.

And when inside there's the concentration required playing video games in hopes to acquire the one-upmanship award. There's also the many types of social media that vies for its place during the normal activities attached to everyone's life. It's either Facebook, Pinterest, YouTube, Twitter, FaceTime, numerous blogs...to name a few.

But no matter what, I achieved great joy watching and listening, and even on occasion, being part of all the internal and external activities in this, our piece of Nirvana...until recently.

Today, June 6, 2020, as I stand watch from my perch, the streets are practically empty and void of many human sightings. And the silence is deafening.

What happened to the joviality, camaraderie, fellowship...from heart to heart and home to home sweet home? And why does everyone look so worried? And why is everyone covering up their smile?

The world has morphed and evolved into myriad eyeballs peering at you from noseless and mouthless faces. Even the family I own stares at me with emotions that are near tears and asking the question, "What's gonna happen to us today?"

No one rubs my belly anymore or scratches the top of my head or gets excited when it's time to take me for a walk.

Voices that used to talk with gaiety oozing from every word now speak in hushed tones of trepidation. And I can't figure out why the grown up people no longer leave the house in the morning and come home in the evening. They're here all the time now. And why did the kids stop going to school?

It was fun at first having everybody at home. I didn't have to wait all day for my potty break. Treats and tussling in the floor games came more often...until I heard my family complaining that we'd almost run out of toilet paper, and couldn't find any Clorox or Lysol products in the store for the fifth week in a row. And I keep hearing and seeing this funny looking little guy on TV talking about some type of "COVIDronademic". And what is this new big word being added to everybody's vocabulary...quarantine?

Hmmmmmmm. Could that be the cause of so much sadness and uncertainty going on in the world right now? Am I watching the results of leadership that's unable to lead well...of an "every man for himself" attitude attached to what should be a united front working to find a workable solution...of the unraveling of what has been perceived, worldwide, as a great nation that is being exposed as a fraud and legend in their own mind?

I don't know what's gonna happen to the family I own or our little neighborhood, nor the world as a whole. Will normal ever be normal again? Will the career of an undertaker become the most lucrative? Will Lysol and Clorox wipes ever appear on the store's shelves again? Will a variety of face masks become the most popular stocking stuffer at Christmas time?

I guess I'll just sit here on my perch and keep looking out my bay window and watch what I can see.

****** Author's note ***** ~ On the date (Sunday September 6th, 2020) that I submitted my "Wally Watchdog" article/story to Jim, our editor, I found the following statistics and information on CNN and Google: COVID/pandemic cases worldwide 26.9+ million…recovered 17.9+ million…deaths 880,000+. USA cases 6.2+ million…recovered 3.41+ million…deaths 188,000+. It's predicted that the USA could have over 410,000 deaths by January 1, 2021. And currently, 29.2 million American workers are now receiving unemployment benefits.*

I don't know what our world will look like in the next six to twelve months. I don't know what will be required of each of us to do our part to help restore the quality of life. But I pray that we put our differences aside and strive to move forward past the aftereffects of this "COVIDronademic" as a cohesive and united class of people under the umbrella of "Yes we are our brother's and sister's keeper."

Stay encouraged. Stay prayerful. Stay hopeful. And through it all, Stay connected to family, friends, and loved ones…near and far.

The Mice in My Life

by Phyllis Tolen

When I was a child, we lived across from the city dump. Routes 40 and 1 cross in the small town of Marshall, Illinois. West on Route 40 on the north side, only a mile out of town, was the town dump. There was plenty of trash and in addition, citizens would go there for target practice. Plenty of rats and mice found sustenance in the trash. It was teeming with animals.

On the south side of Route 40 across from the dump was the Hogue farm where I lived as a child. Our house was a quarter of a mile back on a lane around a circle drive. The home, built in 1858, was three stories and built into a hill. The front showed three stories, but the back showed only two floors. The cellar was underground. This cool room was filled with crates of all kinds of vegetables. There were cabbages, potatoes, carrots, beets, and yams-all grown in the garden. Shelves held jars of green beans, tomatoes, beets, chicken, beef, and soup. A drain was in the corner.

In 1951 the city of Marshall closed the dump. All those mice and rats were happily gnawing away at the remaining garbage. Across the highway, we started a small dump where we burned our trash. Some animals relocated to this second dump.

The kitchen, dining room, laundry, and furnace room were attached to the cellar on the first floor. Our family slept on the second floor. When I was eight years old, I received a beautiful pink sugar egg from the Easter Bunny. It was too pretty to eat, so I displayed it on a shelving unit in the hall. I awoke one morning soon after Easter to find my legs bloody and covered with bites. I must have slept very hard not to have felt the bites under my covers. We also found teeth marks on that tasty egg. It was scary to realize that a mouse or rat had been in my bed. These animals had come up the drain through the cellar, the furnace room, the laundry room, the kitchen, the living room, up the stairs, into the hall and found me, a nice tasty morsel, fast asleep in my bed. Yum, yum.

My dad tried to solve the rodent problem by stuffing rugs under the doors of all of the rooms. He also threw out my beautiful pink Easter Egg. I was more upset about my egg than worried about my bloodied legs.

On the farm, one of my duties was to get the eggs from the nests in the hen house. The feeder was V-shaped with a long tray at the bottom. Often the feed would cake into a solid chunk instead of falling into the tray. Then I would take a hoe and hit the side of the feeder hoping the feed would fall down. Sometimes I was lucky, but sometimes I would lift the lid and poke the feed until it fell down into the tray. Any of these actions led to mice and or rats scurrying out of the top and bottom of the feeder to find safety under the roost or out the door. The hens would run cackling and flying every which way. I hurried out as fast as I could. The mice would run right back into their restaurant that always provided them with food.

Because we lived on a dairy farm, we had outdoor cats of all ages. The farm was the perfect place for them to get milk. My dad actually squirted fresh milk directly from the cow's teat into the cats' mouths and filled an old skillet for them. At one time I counted at least thirty cats and several dogs.

As I grew older, I studied in the kitchen after my family had gone to bed. As a high school student, I sat at the table and did my homework. Our kitchen had a wall of painted white cabinets. The upper cabinets had glass doors, but the lower ones had drawers, doors, and a flour bin. This was a V-shaped drawer that pulled out at the top. My mother stored bags of flour and sugar along with any large containers of foods. Often while I studied, I heard scratching sounds. When I opened the bin, a mouse would try to climb up the slanted side.

Once, after hearing the rustling sounds in the flour bin, I had a great idea. I let a cat inside and pulled the bin open. It worked out great. The cat jumped directly into the bin, grabbed the mouse, and ran out the door with the tail dangling from its mouth. It got to be a habit and the cats would wait outside until I opened the kitchen door and ran in to get the treat.

Several years later, when I graduated from college, I began teaching in another small town called Oakland, Illinois. My husband built a cage for two mice that I bought for the students. One mouse was white, and the other mouse was black. I filled the cage with straw and made a tray for food and water. The local veterinarian came to vaccinate them while the children watched and asked questions. The exchange was educational for the third graders.

One day after lunch as I read to the children, there was a ruckus in the back of the room. "Squeak! Squeak!" Everyone turned to look at the cage.

Spencer, a delightful freckled boy who wore thick glasses, said, "Don't worry. They are just fathering."

The students turned back to look at me and I continued to read. The students were all farm kids and it was nothing unusual.

Soon the children were instructed regarding the care of the mice. There were rules for playing with them, but they could treat them as pets. They played with them at recess when they couldn't go outside. They drew pictures of them, wrote about them, fed, and watered them. One day as I was teaching, I noticed Spencer's pocket was moving.

"Spencer." I said calmly. "What is in your pocket?"

"I didn't get a turn at recess," he said tearfully. He put the mouse back in the cage.

One day I came to school to find the father mouse dragging straw into a pile to make a nest. Soon six babies were born--white, black, and spotted. The children were so excited. A few days later however, there were only four. This created lots of questions. The first one was, "Where did the other two go?" To answer, I explained that sometimes the parents eat the babies that die or are ill-formed or too small to live. I knew that fact from the sows that had baby pigs on our farm.

Another question was, "If a black person and a white person get married and have a baby, will it be spotted?" This was the perfect time to explain about the science of genes. These children had not seen many black people, so it was an interesting learning lesson.

At the end of the school year, I was trying to figure out how to get rid of the mice. The kids were so fond of them that they began asking questions about the mice's future. They had told their parents all of the stories throughout the year. I decided to send home a letter that both parents had to sign if their child could take one home. Strangely. I got several requests back and held a raffle to draw the winners. All six found homes.

My husband and I joined the Peace Corps in 1966. We were assigned to Tacloban, Leyte in the Philippines. I was assigned to Leyte Normal School to teach English as a Second Language. There it was not unusual to see dogs roving and rats and mice scurrying from hiding place to hiding place. I had more than fifty students in each class. It was a big job. I also trained teachers and had fun coaching a debate team. We faced varying types of issues each day. Huge spiders and giant roaches were commonplace in the homes, and were constantly on the lookout for roach eggs in the cupboard. We also slept naked on a thin mattress on the floor. Naked was necessary, because it was so hot that that was the only way to get any sleep. We had a bed, but it was a square wooden frame with woven rattan in the center. The rattan made designs on our bodies and the wooden frame caused us to roll to the center causing pain where the wood struck our bodies.

One night as I lay sleeping on our mat, I felt something crawl across my backside. I thought that a mouse had found me until my husband shone the light on it. It was a giant spider! Don kept a squirt bottle of spray by our mat for this emergency. He squirted the spray and hit the spider which died immediately.

The college there had dances much as we had in the USA. The students had a band and danced the night away. When we attended our first dance, I was surprised to see my students bringing something wrapped up in newspaper. I soon discovered that the entrance fee to the dance was mouse and rat tails. These animals were that common. In addition, the rat and mouse problem was decreased by everyone's entrance fees.

After leaving Peace Corps, I came to New Lenox to teach. I was assigned to third grade at Haven School. Kids brought their lunches each day except on days when the Parent Teacher Organization made barbeque lunches. The sandwiches were served with potato chips and a drink. Some kids didn't want their chips, so I put them in our closet. That way if someone forgot their lunch, a student would share their sandwich and I could give them a package of chips. One day I went to the closet for chips. I noticed a dirty looking circle on one bag. When I picked it up, I saw that it was a black hole. A mouse had gone in and out leaving the dirt from its fur in a circle. I had to set traps in that closet from then on.

There were eight teachers in the building where I taught. Next to me was my friend, Pearl. One day when she came in, she opened her desk's lap drawer. A mouse jumped out into her lap and ran squeaking across the floor. We had to be careful not to leave candy in our drawers. Mice were often seen everywhere, and at one point, we found a dead one in the desk drawer.

My sister grew up afraid of mice. She says she had trouble sleeping because she could hear the mice scratching in the walls. My parents eventually moved to another old house. My mother passed away and my father remarried. My husband and I, along with our lovely daughter, often visited this farmhouse, especially for holidays. One year, our daughter and her husband created a squirrel feeder from a board with a nail sticking up. We often put an ear of corn on the nail and watched the squirrels as they ate the corn directly from the cob.

My father saved a box of corn still on the cob from the fields as a gift for our daughter for her squirrel feeder. He stored the box on the closed in porch. On Christmas Eve we were ready to open gifts, so Dad brought the box inside and placed it under the tree. Everyone was gathering round and suddenly a mouse ran out of the box of corn straight across my sister's foot. It must have sensed how afraid she was. Everyone was shouting and my daughter smacked my sister's foot. My sister screamed and hit my daughter on the arm while she jumped up on a chair. My stepmother then grabbed a broom. At the same time my father opened the kitchen door and she shooed the mouse outside. The cats were waiting. Mice had chewed the corn in the box while it was on the porch. The box had lots of teeth marks and there was a quantity of mouse pills in the box. My sister was so frightened that she only remembers that my daughter played a trick on her and made her "think" that a mouse had run across her foot.

In that same house one year, as we were cleaning, I found a complete skeleton of a mouse upstairs in a bedroom. Its little paw was caught between two floorboards. Nothing but the bones remained. Perhaps another mouse carried the rest away. I put it in a matchbox. My daughter shared it in her anatomy class, and I thrilled my fifth graders with it. I stored it in my desk drawer at school. One day I looked for it, but it was gone. It must have run away.

Many years later my husband got the opportunity to build our own house. The New Lenox Lumber Company put up the shell and we did all of the rest of the work. My husband was very firm about his rules. One was that there should be no food inside of the walls during construction. He didn't want any varmints inside. That plan was successful except that sometimes we left the garage door open. Then some mice would sneak into the garage or his shop. He made quick work of them. We lived there for over forty years until he died. I finally had to move to a townhouse.

My daughter visits me for a couple of days each month. This year the whole family visited me at Thanksgiving, but at Christmas she wanted me to go to their house. She came to pick me up and stayed to help me do a few things before we left for Ohio. First, we ate some microwave popcorn. I cleaned up the kitchen. I threw the buttery bag into the trash can under the kitchen sink. She went to bed early since she is used to Ohio time, which is an hour ahead of Illinois time. So I sat down in the kitchen to play a few games at the computer. In a little while I heard some paper rustling. It sounded like it was under the sink. I quietly opened the cabinet door. It was a mouse chewing the popcorn bag. I had never had any mice in this house but the weather had turned cold. My house backs up to a corn field. I thought I could trap it in the trash can but it raced away to safety under the sink. The next morning we set traps armed with peanut butter under the sink, in the laundry and near the refrigerator. My daughter crawled under the sink with some caulk and put it around all of the pipes that entered and exited there. We caught eight mice in one day, disposing of them outside. We left the next day for Christmas in Ohio and asked my neighbor to watch the house.

When we returned after Christmas, my friend had caught three more in our absence. Eleven mice. Oh my!! I began to remember the mice in our house when I was a little girl. I worried about how many more there might be. When we had the bathroom remodeled a few weeks before Christmas, the contractor said a dead one fell out of the ceiling when he took the fan down. He also mentioned there were plenty of droppings in the attic.

After my daughter went home to Ohio, I had lots of

newspapers to read so I sat down in my nice comfortable chair to catch up on my reading. I turned on the TV to multi-task. After being with the family for Christmas, it was pleasant to have a quiet evening alone. All of a sudden, I was aware of something strange. I felt a light touch on my shoulder. I slowly looked out of the corner of my eye. There, on my left shoulder were two beady eyes staring at me.

ANOTHER MOUSE!!!!! I thought I could hit it but when I moved it ran. I set one of the traps on the floor behind my chair. Within fifteen minutes the trap went off. The mouse had returned. I think he wanted me to adopt him. I took hold of his tail and dumped him outside, hoping he was the last one. I have had enough mouse visits to last a lifetime, so I called an exterminator who set traps and put poison in the basement, the attic, the garage, and under the sinks. He assured me they would not smell. I have not seen nor heard another mouse in my house. Do you think this is the end of my story? I sure hope so.

A Lesson Learned

by Diane Perry

Every day after work, I take my precious friend, Ashlee, around the circle of our development for a fifteen-minute walk. Cesar Milan, famous dog whisperer and dog psychologist, expresses the importance of exercise for a dog. The best way to show you are a pack leader is by exercise, discipline and affection – in that order.

One day when passing a home on our walk, a French bulldog pushed open the fence gate of his yard.

"Rah, rah, rah," as he growled viciously running for my dog. The bulldog flipped Ashlee on her side and was biting her underside ferociously. However, the skin didn't break because of her muscular body.

As I scurried to shield her, yet not knowing what to do, I lifted my fifty-seven-pound Labrador above my waist. As her weight weakened my arms, I slowly lost the battle of holding her up.

I screamed, "Help, help" as the dog owner stood nearby ignoring me as she chatted with her neighbor over the fence.

I screamed even louder, "Help me, help me," as my voice cracked in frustration.

Finally, the neighbor saw what was going on and ran to my

rescue. She apologized for Tommy's behavior.

"Those furniture movers broke our fence gate, I'm so sorry."

In a concerned manner I asked, "Did your dog receive his rabies shot?" as I looked at the dog with no collar or tags.

She answered, "Yes, he received all his shots for the next three years. Give me your email and I will forward his vaccine information to you."

My husband and I gave the email address. Minutes later, we received the record of the vaccine on our phone.

The next week, Ashlee and I were enjoying our walk as Tommy broke out of his home by pushing the front door open. He ran after Ashlee growling viciously, "Rah, rah, rah."

I kicked at him and yelled, "He's running after us. Help, help."

As we ran into the street, the owner planting her flowers ran to us yelling, "Tommy, Tommy," as she grabbed her dog pulling him away. "I am so sorry; he is fine with other dogs but doesn't like black dogs because a dog this color tried to hump him once."

The third time Tommy broke out and attacked Ashlee is when I realized her apologies were fake and called the police.

The policeman came to my door, "I understand you had a complaint about a dog attack."

I said, "Yes, I do. It happened three times already. Every

time I take my dog for a walk, their dog breaks out and bites my dog."

"You can either fine them, or I can give a verbal warning."

"I don't want to fine her, but hopefully a verbal warning will correct this problem."

My husband, coming from the living room, said disgustedly, "All they need to do is fix their gate. I don't know why they can't do this."

The officer said nothing, but continued to write.

After the verbal warning was given, I was confident the warning would help. Yet Tommy broke out again, and again being the fifth time.

As Tommy ran after Ashlee, I grabbed him and pinned him down like Cesar Milan taught me in his many videos. Although my puffy coat shielded me, I was shaking with anger. As I held him by his doggie sweater, I pulled him away from my face.

I held Tommy on my right and Ashlee on my left, as the two dogs looked at each other. Every time Tommy looked at Ashlee I said, "Don't look at her. She is a good girl." I wanted them to smell each other and be friends.

A lady walking along with a baby carriage yelled from a distance. "Do you need some help? Looks like you have your hands full."

I answered in relief, "Yes, could you let this house know their dog is out?" as I motioned with my head to the house across the street.

The passer-by nodded and walked up to the door of Tommy's house. Tommy's owner, behind the door looked at me, then sent her daughter out to retrieve the dog in her embarrassment.

The little girl with her Dorito bag ran to her dog. She said, "Tommy, what are you doing?"

Tommy in his submission trembled after he saw the girl. He whimpered and said, "Roo," like Scooby-Doo in the cartoon show as if he apologized for his behavior.

I told the girl, "You need to walk Tommy. He needs to release some energy." What I was thinking was, "This stupid dog needs to go to Cesar's dog psychology center." I was shaking from the situation yet felt confident I was able to handle the two dogs by the lesson Cesar taught me.

After these redundant events, I called the police once again to file a complaint. After thirty minutes, the police officer's car arrived at my house and he walked up to my door.

He said, "I am here about a dog complaint."

"Yes officer, this time I want my neighbor to pay the seventy-five-dollar fee. It has happened one too many times already."

He wrote up the ticket, handed it over to me and I signed it.

Weeks later, I found out the ticket was paid by the due date.

As the autumn season arrived a month later, Scott and I took Ashlee for a walk in the evening. As we passed Tommy's home, there he was running after my dog once again. "Rah, rah, rah."

My husband pushed him away per Cesar's lesson of putting your hand in a fist to push the dog away. This is the response another dog exhibits to show a dog who the pack leader is. This action doesn't cause harm, but leadership. My husband portrayed the pack leader dog.

As the dog ran away, his owner yelled, "Tommy, do you want some pepperoni?" Tommy ran further away in a distance as his owner ran after him.

Innocent, aggressive dogs are euthanized every year because of arrogant, lazy people who don't invest their time to train. Cesar stresses two twenty-minute walks per day to release energy. Discipline is encouraged to designate who the pack leader is. The practice of turning the dog upside down in submission will release more energy. The dog will growl and fight until tiring, then lie still. This means he has submitted to you. When the dog is still and calm, this is the time to show affection as the reward.

Tommy is a smart dog; he learned all the lessons we taught him. Unfortunately, his owners couldn't be taught a damn thing. Cesar would have shaken his head at this scenario. Many people don't understand a dog's psychology as they keep reinforcing a behavior that they don't know is wrong. Pepperoni was given for a bad behavior. A reward should only be given when a dog is in a calm-submissive state of mind.

Animal Behavior

by Sylvester Kapocius

The people I knew or dealt with in the past who had a dog, believed a full-breed was a better dog to own than a mixed breed. Full breeds were considered smarter and always obeyed commands. However, most folks did not purchase dogs at all. They were either given one by a friend or relative, or took a stray in off the street. Most people owned mixed breeds. People I knew all had dogs with a mild behavior pattern. Back in the Thirties, some raised hunting dogs and hunted with them.

A question often arose among dog owners: Was a full-breed dog better to own than a mixed? Which was more obedient and obeyed commands? Which was a better watchdog? Owners proudly bragged about their dogs when a conversation started.

I only knew a few who owned full-breed dogs. Since mixed-breed dogs were in most of my life, I enjoyed each one I owned or became acquainted with.

My brother Ben had more contact with dogs than me. He knew more about them than I did. He theorized about their behavior and played with them more than me.

He told me one day, "Don't ever raise your hand above a dog's head, they may feel threatened. Open the palm of your hand below their chin; they will be curious to see what is offered to them."

My wife, Betty, is called "The Cookie Lady" in our neighborhood. Not only is she generous to the children she knows, but also to the dogs that know her. When she asks the dog, "Do you want a cookie?" the dog jumps up to kiss her. That seems to me the only way a dog can reply to her question is to bark and to jump up and kiss her.

My friend, Steve, had many dog friends. His folks ran a small food store. Stray dogs always found that store because of the litter from candy bars, ice-cream wrappings, and uneaten food remnants strewn on the ground. It was a daily janitorial duty assigned to Steve – he had to keep the area clean. Whenever some dogs came around with an ugly behavior or unhealthy condition, Steve called the Animal Control Center. They came, took charge, and hauled the dog away.

On occasion, Steve would come across a dog that appeared to be the kind he would want as a pet.

One day, it happened. He and a dog fit together as friends almost immediately. He asked his dad if he could keep him. His dad answered, "We will let him sleep in the shed tonight, and we will take it from there tomorrow."

That made Steve so happy. He fed him and taught him to obey commands. Then one customer at the store said to Steve, "That might be somebody's dog, and it got lost and they might be looking for him right now."

That really shook up Steve. As I stood there, I said to him,

"That's right, Steve, you do not own that dog yet. But in the meantime, what name will you call him by?"

He said, "Skippy. I picked that name for him the first day I saw him. I hope no one claims him, he is mine right now."

Each animal seems to shape its own lifestyle. It needs to eat, so it will search and explore for food. It may fashion his own  environment by himself or with a mate. A wild animal, out in the open, makes its own limits. A caged animal knows its limits. Since it is aware that his home and food are donated by his owner, he will cater to him. It is his best and only choice.

I have been to the Brookfield Zoo, a zoo in Wisconsin, another one in Missouri, and the Will County Fairground in Peotone, Illinois. Out of all those, I liked Peotone the best. It was open in August each year. I was able to have close contact with many animals in their shelters. I petted them as I walked past their stalls. I watched a man sheer the wool from sheep. I saw how a young lad, who was a member of the 4H Club, gave his horse a scrub-down with a water hose and a brush.

A contest took place among different age-levels of boys and girls from the club. They entered to see who handled their horses best by commands. The winner received a colored ribbon.

When I walked through my neighborhood every day, I saw many homeowners owned dogs – over half the subdivision. Almost all were mild-tempered. They wagged their tails when they approached me. That is a happy dog. It must have lived in a good home. What I gathered in my mind was who taught it to behave so well? Others were mean, and I wondered how that happened.

My dog was my pet, and I treated him like a family member.

Most kids I knew attached to dogs very quickly when they were first acquired. They wanted a nice little puppy and promised their parents they would care for them. But how long did that last when it came time to take it out for a walk, feed it, or clean up after it made a mess. If someone is a real pal to his dog, caring for all its needs is not too difficult a chore.

In one animal park, which we visited several times, the animals were always hungry. At first, I wondered why. Later, it dawned upon me.

If they were well-fed, they would not come close to visitors to be petted. Food vending machines were placed around the park for visitors to purchase food to feed them.

One time, with our car window open, a moose stuck his head through the open window and snorted around inside as he sniffed for food. I could not raise the window to close it. He was satisfied with his search and removed his head after a few seconds. That was a bit scary.

At the start of each one of our camping trips over a period of twenty years, our dog, Tipper, during his seventeen-year life, recognized the word, "Camping." If that word was whispered, he heard it. His ears perked up, he ran over next to me, and excitedly jumped up and down because he knew I was the driver. He did not settle down until he plopped down in a chosen corner of the vehicle as I drove off.

When we got to camp, wherever it was, mainly on some waterfront, he jumped around the vehicle as we unloaded. After camp was set up, we all headed for a dip in the cool water.

He was always the first one in.

Then it was a boat ride some time later.

I was so glad that Tipper was a real water sport. If any of us walked toward the water, at any time, he was right with us.

One of his favorite parking places was near or on top of the boat so we would not forget to take him with. He participated in all our functions, and received so many compliments from strangers for being such a cute dog.

When we were in our twenties, Betty begged me many times to take her horseback riding. Well, that day came. Betty, my brother Ben, my friend Rich and I drove up to a farm near Antioch, which was popular among horseback riders.

The owner asked us if we were all riders. Ben, Rich and I immediately popped up with a, "Yes," but Betty did not. Right then I thought about her silence. Jack, the owner, thought he heard us all say yes, so he brought out four horses from the stables. All the horses were about the same size. First-time customers are sized up and assigned a certain horse to ride. Betty was told to get on her horse first. She turned to me and said, "That great big thing, I could never ride it or even get up on it."

Well, Jack heard all of that so he brought the horse back into the stable, brought out a pony, and assigned Betty to a pony-trail ride. She got up on her horse with a big smile and joined that group.

Ben, Rich, and I climbed up on our horses. We had no problem. My brother and I felt comfortable and our horses seemed very comfortable with us, like they knew us forever. But not Rich's horse. His horse was unsettled and bounced around. Rich said, "This horse does not like me. He is even trying to nip me."

We told Rich to show him he is in control, and command the horse with a slight kick in the shins.

Well, that worked at first, so Ben and I rode off across the wide open prairie as fast as we could, like in cowboy western movies.

I stopped and looked back to see Rich. He continued to have problems with his horse. He said, "My horse doesn't want to obey me. He is trying to get me off his back. Look at my face – it's scratched from some low-slung branches of a tree he ran under on purpose, probably to shake me off him."

Rich took his horse in and we followed soon after. Then we talked about the mood of animals relating to people on our way home.

This is when I realized how smart animals are.

Togetherness

by Todd Hogan

Slim, reclusive Christine had mixed feelings when she was furloughed from her job at the library. Many days since the pandemic struck, surrounded by so many people coming and going, she had felt unsafe at work. Though she counted many patrons as friends, what did she know about them, really? Did they always wash their hands, cough into their elbows, and stay a safe distance apart? She had seen evidence of the way some people behaved in the stacks, in the computer rooms, and while gulping a snack or an uncapped drink. Preventing the spread of germs was not a high priority for most patrons.

So when she was let go at the end of March, Christine felt guilty to be so relieved. She rationalized that being home would give her the opportunity to get close to her husband again. Ethan, an advertising executive, worked in Chicago for now. That left Christine alone in their suburban home. She might be alone, but she was comfortable. Her neighborhood felt like a private warren, her own Watership Down. She treasured her personal library of books and videos but missed the usual excitement of exploring a new, unknown book or discovering a young author.

On weekends, she complained to Ethan while brushing her long hair, the color of dark chocolate. "What books should be next on my list? Who will I discuss my books with? I'm kind of lost here.

And we have bees in the bathroom."

Ethan looked at her from the side of his eyes before answering. "I wish someone would pay me more to stay home than I was paid while working!" He had signed Christine up for unemployment benefits immediately. "Look, we'll save the stimulus checks and the unemployment checks. The markets are bound to rebound. This is the time to invest, especially with money we didn't know we were going to get." On the coffee table, he spread out pamphlets and brochures for new investments but she wasn't interested. "And what bees are you talking about?"

"I've never been on unemployment before, Ethan. I've always worked since high school. Do we really need to take stimulus money? I think a bee came through the vent."

"If they shut down Chicago, I'll be furloughed, too. We'll need that extra income. That bee was likely a one-time thing, I'm pretty sure. Coming to bed?"

"Pretty soon. I'm going to call my mom, make sure she and dad are alright."

Ethan woke before dawn and often took an express downtown. He was at his desk by 7:00 at the latest, designing advertising campaigns, usually for television but increasingly for the internet. He came home late most nights, after entertaining clients or nailing down contracts, and collapsed into bed. Even on those nights Christine had worked until 9:00 at the library, she would often be sound asleep before he arrived. Sometimes several days passed before they got an opportunity to talk. It wasn't ideal but they were working for a common goal, to retire to South Carolina by the time they were forty. They sacrificed for their dream, living in a smallish ranch home in a bedroom community on a cozy cul-de-sac, forgoing expensive vacations, and limiting visits to trendy restaurants to once every other month. Ethan owned a Mercedes to impress his clients. She drove an older Nissan, reliable enough to get to the library and home again.

The first thing that unnerved Christine while she was at home was the pervasive quiet. People stayed indoors. The traffic noise diminished. Occasionally, a distant siren or a helicopter rotor overhead betrayed the transport of a patient to the hospital a few blocks away, but those occurrences were rare. The quiet was so widespread that she could sit outside with a cup of green tea and hear leaves rustling in the neighborhood's tall maple and honey locust trees. She had never noticed those sounds before the pandemic. One time, she heard loud, insistent, exciting music from a neighbor through the yard, but that happened only once. The neighborhood had reverted to a peaceful existence.

She checked the bathroom to see if Ethan had done anything about the bees vent access. He had. Under the vent switch was a notecard, with his handwriting, "Release the Bees!"

"Very funny."

#

Spring encouraged the budding flowers, the blossoming

trees, the warming breezes. She had never paid much attention to her neighbors, who were a good mix of ages and backgrounds. Three younger families moved on to the street with their invigorating bunch of little kids. Several older women lived with their younger families but needed to be pushed in wheelchairs or steadied in walkers. One widower received meals on wheels daily. Another poor guy took dialysis twice a week. The cul-de-sac was large enough that everyone minded their own business. However, when a thundershower knocked down branches, everyone pulled together to clear driveways and storm drains. Rob and his pretty strawberry-haired wife from across the street helped all the elder neighbors to clear their sidewalks. Afterward everyone retreated back home. A gentle routine settled in. After supper, the younger girls came out to play. Too young for roller blades, their spindly legs propelled scooters and bicycles, their innocent hair trailing in the breeze. Nevertheless, everyone was back inside by the time the streetlights pulsed on.

While the usual human activity decreased, Christine noticed animal activities surged. She saw more robins gathering on the wires, fences, and evergreen trees. Squirrels' frenetic activity amused her as they chased each other, first just one chasing another, then in groups of three or more. Each time they stopped, their gray tails twitched, commanding attention like naval semaphores. Christine's imagination provided slapstick plots for the squirrels as lurid as the Rape of the Sabine Women, leaving her laughing as they leapt from branch to branch and spiraled up and down the tree trunks. Pests increased. She saw more rabbits than ever. As a precaution, she spread cayenne pepper around her foundation to discourage skunks from burrowing a den beneath her porch.

Then came the best surprise--the number of scarlet red cardinals that flew into the yard, posed for a few seconds, and lifted off again.

One soft, early morning, Christine sipped green tea on her backyard patio. A red fox slipped from the bushes and paused for a moment. It had a smart russet coat, white paws, and black-tipped ears, which flicked forward and back. It was as slick and groomed as Ethan going off to work. Then the fox trotted silently across her backyard and around the side of her house. It disappeared so quickly, Christine didn't have time to take its photo to show Ethan. She'd never seen a fox in her yard before. There were reports of coyotes along the roads in some areas. But this sighting was so unusual, she wondered if she had actually seen the beautiful creature. The quiet in the neighborhood must be encouraging the wild creatures. Christine could imagine how this area might have looked long before automobiles, generators, powered lawn mowers, and motion-detection lights. The general sense of calm in the neighborhood affected her deeply. She decided to forgive Ethan for the notecard in the bathroom.

As Summer approached, Christine noticed that like the squirrels, there was some frenetic human activity. The red-head across the way entertained a construction worker who stopped by while Rob was away. They were both very young and so Christine supposed they could make those mistakes and still recover. She wondered how anyone would go about finding a lover when everything was shut down. She shook her head and muttered, "No bees in that powder room."

In late June, the inevitable occurred. Ethan was laid off. He spent the first few days cursing his fate, talking on the phone to anyone who would take his call, and stomping in the yard. Christine let him stew and did not let his nervousness affect her sense of calm. Ethan couldn't sit still. He needed projects to work on. In the first few weeks, he cleaned out the garage, reorganized the basement, painted the bedrooms, but stayed away from the bathroom vent. She let him proceed with his organizing, until he began to tell her how to rearrange her library. The final straw came when he made suggestions for how to set up her kitchen moe efficiently. She banished him from the kitchen except for meals.

A tentative peace remained in her small part of the world. Not even an early summer tornado that knocked out the electricity for most of the city upset her equilibrium. The neighbors worked together again. Rob shared his generators with them. Ethan dug out the camping lanterns for those who needed a little light, keeping one for Christine and himself. Those electricity-free nights were darker and quieter than ever. The rabbits scuttled continually over their yard, oblivious to threats from foxes or other predators.

About four o'clock in the darkest part of one night, Christine was startled awake by a scream. She sat up at a right angle and strained to listen for a minute. Was someone strangling a puppy? She shook Ethan from his deep sleep. He listened, too. Then, he smiled.

"That's a fox. That's the sound they make when they're making baby foxes."

"No!" Then she laughed.

"Oh, yes. It's stopped now." He put his hand on Christine's shoulder, and pulled her closer for a kiss. Okay, she thought. It was the first kiss they had shared since he'd been furloughed. She relaxed into his arms and saw him smile.

Encouraged, he slipped off her nightgown and kissed her again. Then he lifted her from their bed with a large blanket and carried her in his arms from the bedroom, through the living room, past the dark, poorly organized kitchen, and to the back door.

"What are you doing, Ethan?"

He held her closer. "No one will see. Come on."

"You're crazy!"

"Shh," he whispered.

The night was warm, humid, and close. Christine knew the yard was shielded by trees and bushes for privacy. Still, she would die if anyone owned a flashlight and saw them. She hugged Ethan tightly around the neck, forcing herself closer to him. He embraced her and kissed her eyelids.

A thin sliver of a moon permitted stars to peek through the veil of night. A slight puff of night breeze raised goosebumps on her skin. Christine had never been so brazen before. For God's sake, she was a librarian! Or at least, she was before the furlough. She kissed Ethan back, hard. He growled, low and purring.

Afterward, they lay giggling, naked under the canopy of leaves provided by a tall tree. Christine felt wild and free. She was one with the sky, the earth, the trees, and the flowers. She enjoyed lovemaking with her husband, her beautiful, strong husband. She was no longer concerned whether anyone saw her, at least not so much any more. She wanted to dance. So, she did, until Ethan covered her with the blanket and led her back to the house. They had never been so reckless as to risk public indecency but she hoped it would not be the last. When they closed the back door, her shoulders slumped. Ethan guided her to the bedroom where they collapsed onto their bed. Ethan fell asleep, but Christine's eyes remained open. She breathed shallowly, looking at the ceiling. She let her breath out slowly and it buzzed between her lips.

The electricity was out for only fifty hours but everyone realized how much they took the convenience for granted. When it came back on, it brought with it a strong impulse to return to some normality. More and more, people clamored to return to work. They were willing to risk whatever illness might be out there for the opportunity to gather again. Ethan was eager to push the envelope. He took up playing golf--"We're socially distant because we're just not that good!"--and even rejoined weekly poker games. He was shocked when three of the eight regular players tested positive, but those three were older guys and all but one did recover.

"That's it!" Christine said. "No more poker. No more golf. The governor has prohibited those gatherings anyway."

Increasingly, Ethan spent his days brooding, sitting on the front porch, watching the neighborhood. "I need something to do, a game plan."

"You always wanted a deck. You could build one of those." Christine asked. "Have you seen the cardinals?"

He shook his head.

"I saw a fox one time. And you have to have seen the crazy squirrels," she said.

"I've seen tons of rabbits bouncing around. That's it. Nothing else. Oh, and our neighbor across the street has a friend that stops by after lunch. I wonder if Rob knows about his wife's construction projects."

"It's not our business, Ethan. Stay out of it."

"I'll just watch the rabbits then." His eyes locked on the small, fluffy, brown balls of fur ambling across the lawn. Christine saw a predator's glare in his eyes. She left him alone.

The next afternoon, a single streamlined streak flew across their front yard. It reminded her of a small electric train, compact, powerful, incessant, and unstoppable. It was an impressive hawk, the first she had seen so closely. It didn't slow or change direction but was single-minded in its search for prey. The most frightening aspect of the hawk was the ebony of its eyes. She perceived an intelligence behind those eyes, but it could not be penetrated. She would hate to be prey targeted by those eyes.

Before dinner, Ethan at the front window called quietly to her. "Come here! Look across the street."

Christine saw the construction worker run from her neighbor's front door, buckling his belt and carrying his shirt. The young red-head was at the front door, wearing only a black bra and panties. She yelled at the man and threw one heavy shoe at him, then the other. She was sobbing, but Christine heard her say, "I hate you. Get out! You bastard. I hate you!" Christine pulled Ethan away from the window, her way of giving her neighbor some privacy and an opportunity to regain some of her dignity.

Ethan prowled their yard after dinner. They hadn't revisited their backyard tryst since the first time. Christine hoped that the lockdown would end soon since she needed a respite from her husband's indifference.

One evening while she was on the couch sipping tea and re-reading Trust Exercise by Susan Choi, she was surprised when Ethan towered over her. His eyes seemed impenetrable as he watched her, making her feel uncomfortable although she was fully clothed.

"I'm not complaining," he began, "but have you ever thought

about plastic surgery?"

"What?!"

"Nothing's wrong, but a lot of people are using this downtime for self-improvement. We can't go to the gym but I was just wondering..."

"Go away, Ethan."

"Just think about it, okay?"

"And what should I think about? Fuller lips? Botox-ed forehead? No, wait. You want me to have bigger boobs. You are so disgusting."

"I've never complained about your chest. It's certainly better than some. I just thought that as long as you're home with nothing to do..."

"How big do you want them, Ethan? Give me an example of someone you think I should emulate."

"Oh, no," he said, shaking his head. "I'm not falling into that trap. Just forget it. I was just thinking."

"Well, stop thinking. I'm going to bed. You should sleep in the guest room tonight, I think."

Christine had trouble sleeping that night. Ethan heeded her advice and slept in the guest room. She arose early, when the sun was just splitting the night into a new day. From her bedroom window, she looked out, hoping to see her handsome fox. Instead, she saw the majestic hawk standing on her front lawn, ebony eyes sparkling, his beak curved down like an axe. It reminded her of Ethan. It was regal, dangerous, but in command of its environs. She hadn't noticed the brown ball of fur beneath its yellow claws until the hawk's head dipped and rose, pulling a string of intestines from the creature beneath it. Her stomach lurched at the sight. Later in the day, Ethan would have to remove the rabbit's remains with a shovel.

She heard Ethan in the bathroom shower. She didn't know what to say to him anymore. He certainly didn't know what to say to her. She peeked in. The bathroom was clouded by the steam. He must have noticed the door move, because he called out to her, "Come on, babe. There's plenty of room in here."

She snaked her arm into the bathroom and found the vent switch which no longer had the notecard below it. She switched it on. Above the hum of the fan, she heard a battle cry in her head, "Release the bees!"

Mornings Mourning

by Paula Morris Thomas

The morning routine I used to have is now gone and I'm wondering where now do I shift my emotions.

Familiar was favorable because it helped to identify me in my purpose and role for my faithful companion and friend.

I'd leave him in the morning and though the essence of the house echoed only his existence, he had his TV and snacks to comfort him until we'd be reunited in what life has fondly titled afternoon/evening.

While away from him I wondered how his day was going...did he need me...did he need anything...had I left him set up with the best self-care he could maneuver until I could get back there...home...our house.

And I knew each day when I returned to him in the afternoon/evening and looked at his countenance that yes, I had done right for my companion, my buddy, my friend. I had done my best...and it had paid off and made the difference for him during our time of separation.

And when what used to be a quality of life showed up as mere shreds of what was, I had to make the tough decision of allowing him to leave with the little flavor of dignity his life still contained...and I did so in love because I knew that the inevitable had come.

Death is a cruel assignment of life.

I miss my Friend.

It feels strange that the TV is no longer on when I leave the house.

Yes...the morning routine I used to have is now gone and I find myself now wondering where now do I abode my emotions.

I think I'll house them in memories and sadness until morning gladness comes again...because it will come again...as just memories.

RIP Rex.

A New Leaf is Turned

by Eric J. Stiltner

As time goes on
The memory fades
But you're always in my heart
A cherished love
On borrowed time
Though our souls will never part

As the seasons change
A new leaf is turned
But I can't help how I feel
Turning back the clock
Won't heal the wound
When the pain is all too real

But I must move on
And must stay strong
Even though you couldn't stay
Now my soul feels weak
And this world's grown cold
Since the day you've gone away

I take great comfort
In knowing that you're always
There watching over me
The time for mourning
Has come to pass
And it's time I set you free

Wheeling Animal Magnetism Has No Bounds

by Jolee L. Price

With his last bite of his birthday cake, Uncle Ned looked at me and motioned to THE room. "Kade, I'll meet you in there in a few minutes."

I find myself in the doorway of his model car showcase room. Growing up, he used to tell me, "Son, let's take a grand tour on the town." I always felt I was violating some sort of classic car sanctuary, but my uncle made it fun. We practically lived at his house and twenty-five years later, still do. He's more than an uncle to me and quite the father figure. I always felt blessed to have two fathers growing up.

My uncle's not only a member of a Classic Car Charter, but an avid model car builder and had made dozens throughout the years. I even got to help him; still do sometimes.

He never said why, but his favorite models were ones named after animals. As a child growing up, I thought it was because he was a veterinarian.

Model cars lined shelves. One section was reserved for his "motor safari" as he called it. There was the 1935 SS Jaguar which he said had this animal's characteristics of being fast and nimble. Next to it was a 1967 Ford Mercury Cougar; sleek and stealthy.

A model 1981 Mercury Lynx faced a 1965 Ford Bronco with

all the horsepower you could muster he would tell me.

The 1959 Ford Falcon and 1957 Thunderbird faced each other. He said these cars were like wings beneath one's feet.

Beneath was a 1993 Ford SVT Mustang Cobra, which was a high-performance version of the Ford Mustang. Unc would tell me a cobra was known to be deadly against one in a race.

Set apart by itself was his favorite model of the 1968 Ford Mustang GT. Actor, Steve McQueen drove one in the 1968 movie, Bullitt. I swear my uncle could quote the entire movie verbatim. He loved the movie's iconic car chase scene. We often played that scene out with my uncle of course using the GT model. Sometimes he would let me be "McQueen." He even owns a 68 Mustang GT which he named McQ.

"Ah, there you are. Have a toast with me Kade." He poured two glasses of Jack Daniels.

"No champagne toast?"

Handing me a glass, "No, you don't mess with a man's drink of perfection."

"Well, Happy 80th Unc."

"Indeed, it is, son. Take a seat."

Moments passed in comforting silence.

"Kade, I've been doing the Classic Car shows for years now. You've been my copilot many times."

I set my glass down. "Unc, what's going on? Are you alright?"

"No need to worry, son. The docs say I'm in good shape for a man my age."

Noticing the look on my face, he said, "Now don't you go worrying about me. You know I always shoot straight from the hip; no lies or excuses."

He could say that again. I never got away with anything with him; still don't to which I'm actually grateful. "Nah, I plan to keep on keepin' on until I can't. I'll admit I've slowed some, but that's all. There's plenty of car shows coming up that I'd like to attend. You know how fun they are and how good it is to see the regulars and rookies."

Laughing out loud, I said, "You can say that again. I loved going with you."

"Glad to hear because I'd like to be the copilot from this day forwards with you as my pilot."

I stood up so fast I nearly dropped my drink. "You mean I get to drive "McQ?"

"It's not like you've never driven her, son; besides, you know how to take care of her."

"You taught me well."

I sat back down and said, "To many more shows."

In silence, our glasses clinked in agreement.

Small Animals

by Sylvester Kapocius

They are everywhere. How about the hummingbird? Is that a small animal? It does things different than the other birds. It can remain in mid-air by fluttering its wings more cutely than the rest of its winged family.

One summer, hummingbirds were my daily visitors. While I drank coffee on the back porch after breakfast, enjoying the sight of the rising sun and gentle breeze, all of a sudden I heard the fluttering wings of a hummingbird. It was right next to my ear and sounded like an electric fan. It investigated the coffee cup I held in my hand. It flew to the bird feeder which hung from the porch ceiling. At first it attempted to retrieve sugar from the donut at my lips and then it flew right up to the feeder and got some sugar water.

One afternoon a bright green hummingbird headed right to one evergreen tree. It did not venture to enter between the branches for fear of the sharp needles and flew away. I was surprised to see one that color.

Then came a squirrel. It crept slowly toward the bird feeder which I built on a stand in the back yard. I paid little attention to it and went into the house. When I returned outside, a half hour later, a mess was on the ground all around the stand. Somehow that rascal managed to get right to the feeder and emptied it all.

Something had to be done, and I found a way. I used a design which ships used while they tied to a dock. It was a metal funnel called the rat guard. I often wondered how the rats knew there was food on the ship.

The squirrels were a funny bunch. Those which entered my life, were show-offs and had unpredictable behavior. Squirrel movements are fancy and cute.

You will always see one at an acorn tree. Where many trees grew together, there was a squirrel village. That is what we had near the apartment we lived in. When the frost showed on the ground, acorns carpeted the earth around our building. I collected acorns and filled a cardboard box full. I saved them for the coldest part of the winter. When visitors came with their children, and without toys, they had fun feeding the squirrels with the acorns I picked from the ground. When I brought the box of acorns out, the squirrels were at my feet in seconds. Their begging manners were so cute.

Another time, I watched a squirrel walked on a cable between two poles, thirty feet off the ground. Lightning flashed through the sky and it fell to the ground. It laid there like dead for about ten minutes. It got up on its feet as the rain poured down, then he ran quickly up the tree to his nest.

The flying squirrel, so called, does not fly. The two times I saw one was near our lake house when we lived in Missouri. Both times I saw it must have been the same guy. As I walked down the hill on a gravel road through the woods, I watched the squirrel leap from the branch of a tall tree, smoothly sailed through the air with its webbed legs stretched out, right over me to a branch of a small tree, about a hundred feet away. It was colored brown.

Acorn trees grew all around our apartment. Leaves that fell off those trees piled twenty inches high on the ground in some places. That gave me a lot of work. I raked them up and filled bushels full. Some made compost piles with them. Acorns from all those trees covered the ground everywhere.

During a rainstorm, I saw one leap through the air off of a very high tree branch to another tree's branch, four feet through the air and barely caught it.

When we were pre-teens, we carried a coffee can with us to a park or a cemetery. We filled it with water and looked for an inconspicuous small hole in the ground. We poured water into it and scanned across the surrounding area to see a ground squirrel pop up out of a hole somewhere in the ground from its tunnel. It was so much fun to watch them pop out of one hole and run to another one which led to the same tunnel they lived in.

My brother Ben had a pet canary. It stayed in the house all the time, mostly in the kitchen. Before anyone entered the house, chirping of a bird was heard. It was Skippy, a small yellow canary. He was a happy, happy little bird. It chirped and whistled short tunes all day long.

Ben and my mom wore napkins on their heads in the kitchen

where Skippy flew around most of the time. It took me a while to realize why they covered their heads. It looked silly. Ben let him have his freedom out of the cage for hours. At meal-times, Skippy was on Ben's shoulder and was fed from his hand. That bird ate almost anything. When Ben turned the radio on and listened to music, Skippy chirped loud as ever. I could not determine whether it was in protest or enjoyment. As soon as the music stopped, his chirping stopped immediately, and all was quiet for several minutes, then the chirping began again.

One day some children came to see Skippy. He heard their voices and jumped right up to the cage door. One boy saw his one leg got caught in the cage wire so he pulled him loose. That injured his leg and that poor bird squealed loud as ever. Ben heard it from another room. The leg came off and Skippy laid on his belly at the bottom of the cage. It was sad. Nothing could be done for him. Later in the day, Skippy tried to hop on one leg and fell. The next day it was a surprise to see him hopping around a lot, but Ben held him a lot and he enjoyed that. He chirped more each day and hopped around with the one leg as a normal thing, happily as before. He was two years old when that occurred and the next five years he hopped and hopped on one leg happy until he passed on.

We all missed that happy bird. Ben missed him the most. He never got another bird because he said, " I would never find another bird like Skippy."

THE SMALL TURTLE

It is an animal, it was small, it was a turtle. One pound or so, a snapper. It had a flat back. Most commonly found in mud ponds where I lived.

When I played with my childhood friends at about the age of eight, we all raised some pet. Not cats or dogs but animals, such as a hamster, rabbit, canary, frog, fish, or turtle. I found a small turtle when I waded barefooted through a mud pond which was located in a prairie outside the city of Chicago. I put it in a tin can found on the ground and brought it home. At home I placed it in a large can filled with grass and some water. The kids down the street saw the can I carried and hollered, "Whatcha got, let me see" When they surrounded me, and saw what was in the can, I felt big-time, because I found a snapping turtle. I named him Snappy.

The following day my brother saw what I had and said to me, "You can get salmonella poisoning from it, Dad will know about this."

Dad saw it and said, "Bring it back to where you got it." Well that hurt and did not go well with me so my first thought was to keep it, and I hid it. For a while I hid it under the porch, sometimes behind the garage and even in the far corner inside the basement behind some boxes. It was well fed each day with lettuce and carrots from the fridge. Mom knew but said nothing to dad. I brought it out in the prairie to play with. I fed it and watched how good he snapped at everything that was placed before him. After a while it got boring so I looked for someone who would take it from me.

Ronnie saw me walking down the street with it and asked what I had. He saw the turtle in the can and said, "Can I have him?" I hesitated to hand it over to him because he was the bad kid in the neighborhood and thought he would not be a good pet owner, but I gave it to him.

When I visited him a week later, and saw Snappy's environment, neat as ever, I knew he was in good hands.

Several weeks later, the unexpected happened. Ron called me to see his turtle. It was inactive. At the same time his dad came out and looked at it. Ron asked his dad, "Is he sick?"

The answer was, "Yes, and he might die soon."

As soon as Ronnie heard that he sobbed a bit. Then his dad turned to him and said, "Don't feel bad son. When Snappy passes on, we will place him in a nice cardboard box and bury him in the back yard with a flower over his grave. Then with all the kids on the street, we will have a small lunch and lots of ice cream, cookies and cake."

Then the mean streak popped out of Ron, "Dad, let's kill him."

It did not happen that way, he passed on naturally.

THE LARGE TURTLE

Our ship, the USS Seaflasher, sailed out of the five-foot waves into the two-foot waves, and then slowed onto the smooth but murky water into the Milne Bay, New Guinea. It was April, 1944 during WW-2. No more soothing ocean breeze. The temperature was 115 degrees. The ship stopped moving and anchored in water hardly deep enough, very close to shore. The thickest tropical growth ever, grew right up close to the shoreline. I reeked from the horrible stench which oozed out from heart of the jungle. The thick hot air smelled like a toddy of vinegar and sour wine. Much of it was from scattered litter which remained from the invasion of the Japanese.

When I removed my shirt for the first time crossing the ocean, the mosquitos got on me and had a Banquet with my blood. My shirt went right back on. We had been taking the sour-tasting pill Atabrine for the past week. It was to help prevent a Malaria infection from those blood-suckers that filled the air.

The sun set, we had our last meal for the day. Some found their niche for comfort and settled in for the night. I, and six others grouped together at the ship's port-bow railing. We bragged about our home state, about sports, what we liked to do most, and about the most important people in our lives. Time passed quickly, it got dark, and the ship's lights turned on. It was hot so we went to sleep. Some laid on their life jackets, right on the steel deck, but I went below to my bunk.

The next day it was about the same. It was hot, humid and a short tropical rain showered after noon. Our grop formed together at our assigned stations. It felt good to be up on deck and not below.

Bud came up to me and said, "Let's jump in the water to cool off." Before I could answer him, he threw the climb-back-up rope over the side and jumped down into the water, with clothes and all. He looked up at us and hollered, "Come on you guys, jump on in and join me, the water feels good."

I could not resist, so I jumped in right next to him. We splashed around for several minutes close to the anchor below the bow so the officers at the upper deck would not see us. After a short cool-off period, I said to Bud, "Let's get back up on the ship, its scary down here." Bud climbed the rope first and struggled to reach the railing. When I climbed, I became exhausted about five feet from the top, I wrapped the rope around my ankle and rested. Then I continued my climb with all of my strength and reached the railing with the help of two in the group. After resting, we all went to chow.

Right then, the ship's speakers screeched out loud and an announcement blared out. "Anyone jumping ship will be put in the brig immediately."

Now, how did the officers in the upper deck know that Bud and I jumped overboard in the water if they could not see us from where they were? Everyone was quiet as they stared at Bud and me. I waited for our names to be called out from the speakers, but nothing was heard.

After evening chow it was story-telling-time again at our assigned stations on the ship. There was a lot to talk about, and we stayed up late. It was after midnight. The ship's spotlight went on and focused on the water. A large garbage scow tied up right below us. The tugboat untied and left in the dark. It was quiet as ever. It was a sign we would leave within the next eight hours after the food scraps were removed from our ship.

One standing in our group excitedly said, "Look down there at the barge." I looked down and I saw a large snake, twenty-five feet long with a ten-inch-thick body. It was an Anaconda. It nibbled on the food scraps from the pile. It ate for several minutes, then backed off the barge and slipped away into the murky water.

That was something we talked about for a long time. It was already about 2 A.M. Then I heard a splash in the water. I looked down at the food-scrap-pile on the barge. There was a huge turtle eating the lettuce and carrots scraps from the pile. Half of its body hung off the barge in the water while it clung to the edge of the barge with its huge claws. It was oblivious to our attention. Its body was about six feet long, four feet wide, two feet thick with a neck and claws about ten inches round. As we watched in awe, a huge spotlight turned on from the upper deck and focused directly on the turtle.

Then the speakers blared out, "Now hear this, if anyone cares to cool-off in the water may do so, there is space below the bow of the ship" We all bust out laughing because that was where the turtle was and we knew that announcement was aimed at Bud and me. I just knew the officers on topside heard us laugh.

We all went to sleep. At about five in the morning, I awoke

during a horrible nightmare. I dreamed that the snake slithered next to my body in my bunk. I awoke abruptly and my heart was beating two-forty. In seconds, I felt the ship rocking back and forth. That was a sign we were moving. I went up on deck and saw that we were well on our way with blue skies and water all around.

An Act of Compassion

by James Pressler

I first knew I wanted to become a veterinarian when I was eight. We had a sheepdog, Shep, who lived in our barn and was my best friend even though he was twice my age – over one-hundred in dog years. The black-and-white fur heap slept by the water pump all day, letting sparrows land on his head. He no longer ran around and we didn't play in the fields anymore, but I was happy just to brush him and pet him and watch his tail wag. I was like his little brother in that way.

One weekend, my parents sent me and my little brother to stay with our grandparents for a few days. When we came back, Shep was gone. Our parents said Shep had gotten sick and they had to take him somewhere so he could get better. They told us they took him to this big farm upstate, where he could run through the fields and chase rabbits and play with other dogs, but he couldn't be with us anymore. My little brother started crying, and my parents wept as well. At that moment, I decided I didn't want anyone else to go through what we were going through. I was only eight, but somehow I knew what my parents meant when they talked about that "big farm upstate." If I had my way, nobody's pet would ever have to go there again.

After that, my life trajectory pointed toward becoming a veterinarian. Summer jobs with animals, volunteering at the shelter, everything in my life moved toward that goal. A veterinary degree would be the final step in a journey I started when I was eight. When I took the first course in my major, I sat in the front row of the lecture hall, dead center, so close to the podium that no knowledge would escape my grasp.

That is when I met Dr. Chandra.

She was not what I expected for a professor in veterinary medicine. The tall, elegant Indian woman strode smoothly to the podium, her maroon sari gliding about her as if she drifted in on a breeze, the river of black hair flowing down to her knees. She was peaceful, an air of calm and serenity surrounding her. If blue robins flew in to drape scarves about her, I would not be surprised.

"I have a question for all of you," she began with a clear voice that carried through the hall even before she reached the microphone. "Please answer aloud. In one word, what do you feel is the single most important difference between a doctor who treats people and a veterinarian?"

Plenty of people offered a variety of answers, from the insightful to the ludicrous: Kindness, generosity, paycheck and so forth. I paused until everyone said their word then said in my boldest voice, "Compassion."

Dr. Chandra nodded at the class. "There is no right answer. But for all of you who said something, that is what makes it special to you. Remember that, for it will be the most important part of your career, and indeed, your life."

And just for a second, her eyes caught mine, and she smiled.

I spent my college years doing whatever I could to learn from Dr. Chandra. I studied each syllabus to make sure she was my professor whenever possible. Sometimes, during my spare time, I sat in the back row of her other lectures for courses I had already taken. I became her own personal academic stalker with good intentions and a perfect GPA.

Eventually, I met her during office hours to try and figure out what it was about her I was drawn to. She was old enough to be my grandmother, but exuded an amazing youth when we talked about animals. We talked about classwork of course, but sometimes I would just listen to her discuss the socializing habits of horses, the universality of maternal instincts, or the adventures she had with an endless litany of pets. She loved her animals. That is where we bonded. She had a compassion for every creature around her I had never seen in anyone before or since. In that sense, we were very much the same.

My senior year was a bittersweet time, as I knew I would go into the real world and no longer orbit around Dr. Chandra. The week before finals, she pulled me aside after class and asked if I could be available for a little veterinary mission that weekend. How could I resist? I accepted with abundant eagerness, and that weekend she picked me up and we headed out.

As we left the city in her beige convertible (that much I did not expect), she asked me about my pets back on our farm. I realized in all our time together I had never talked about my experiences, instead just enjoying her many tales. With just the slightest prompting, I started talking about the cows and chickens, the cats and rats prowling through the barn, and how the sparrows would land on Shep. Once I started on about Shep, I just fell into memory.

I was only eight when Shep went to the big farm upstate, yet every story came back to mind in vivid detail. As a toddler, my parents would set me on Shep's back and I would ride him like a horse. I didn't know I could recall anything when I was that young, but that memory felt new and fresh. Sometimes I curled up against Shep's belly and napped on sunny afternoons. Was I just a toddler? Story after story came to mind and I shared each one as best I could. I was no longer sitting in the beige convertible. I was back in the barn, lying within that pile of black-and-white fur.

After my story about how, as a toddler, Shep carried me around by the seat of my pants, I realized I had been talking non-stop for way too long. I looked around to see we had left the city way behind, her car rumbling along a tree-lined country road that followed a wide creek.

"Sorry I went on like that," I apologized. "I got carried away. Where are we?"

"We are approaching my property," she said. "Next turn on the left."

As the road bent around, a side road appeared just as she

said. Dr. Chandra slowed down and pulled up next to the mailbox, pulled out a few papers, then turned onto the little road guarded by two huge trees. She drove over a colorfully painted bridge crossing the creek, following the road beyond to a broad pasture rising up toward a copse of trees with a cabin nestled within. Wildlife filled the property. Cats roamed about in packs, rabbits hopped in and out of the shrubs, and two horses with shiny chestnut coats trotted past the cabin, no halters or saddles visible. It was the perfect animal sanctuary – so clearly Dr. Chandra's place.

"This is beautiful," I said in astonishment. "What veterinary work could you possibly need here?"

"It's the kind of mission that will truly make you a veterinarian."

She pulled up to the cabin, the horses nearby unconcerned about the car. I saw hawks in the trees, scouting the skies even though field mice scurried throughout the undergrowth. As I stepped out of the convertible, one of the horses walked up to me, gently nuzzling my shoulder. I petted his mane, running the soft hair through my fingers.

"Chestnut's always been my favorite color on a horse," I said while sifting through the lustrous hair. "My parents had a picture of two beautiful chestnut horses they used to own, and it hung in the family room. They were splendid, and the picture just hypnotized me. They lost them a year after I was born. They never talked about what happened." I looked into the horse's big, brown eyes. "I guess they never got over losing their pets."

Dr. Chandra approached, handing me a carrot from a bag she grabbed out of the trunk. "Nobody ever truly loses their pets, you know."

I fed the carrot to the big horse, paying more attention to the meal in progress. "I know – the whole 'as long as we remember them, they're never truly gone' line of thinking. I just know it was so tough for them that they never got another horse again. No offense, but they lost those horses."

"Then how can you be feeding one of them?"

I looked at her in confusion. "What do you mean? Did they put their horses out to stud?"

Dr. Chandra smiled. "Don't you know where we are?"

"Your property," I said, no longer sure just what that meant.

"It's more than that." She clapped her hands twice, and I heard something start running through the undergrowth toward us. It burst through the bushes by the drive and came at me full speed.

It was Shep.

As the big sheepdog rushed up to me, leaping up to lick my face, I couldn't speak. I couldn't breathe. This was my big brother-sheepdog just as I remembered him. Energetic and lively, his piles of fur bouncing about even after he stopped running. He was clean, happy, full of life and thrilled to see me. For a dog that had been dead for fourteen years, he looked better than ever.

While holding my best friend again, I turned to Dr. Chandra. "I still don't understand."

"This," she said, spreading her arms wide, "is the big farm upstate – as you might call it. This is where all our beloved pets go to be happy as they wait for us. It's quite a beautiful place, isn't it?"

"So, when my parents say they took Shep to the big farm upstate, they really took him…"

"Your parents had to put Shep down," she answered with a solemn nod. "A sad necessity to ease your fine dog's suffering. And on that day, this fine dog showed up at my property, where he was welcomed to live until you could join him again."

"Wait. Am I dead?"

"No," Dr. Chandra chuckled. "On rare occasions I bring special students with the deepest of compassion across, so they know there is a good place where their beloved pets are taken care of. You're a very special student and will be a wonderful veterinarian. I am offering you this gift so you never doubt your actions and you always know there is a very happy place for your pets – the big farm upstate."

I still hadn't broken my hug from Shep. So much to take in and understand. "So, you're a professor and you take care of Pet Heaven?"

She shrugged, bobbing her head about in neither agreement nor denial. "It's not very difficult."

"And Pet Heaven – the home for all the pets in the whole world – just happens to be an hour outside the city?"

She fed another carrot to the horse. "This isn't any one place. It isn't any place on a map. But this special space is yours, and now that you've been here, you can return any time. Every animal you've ever shared your time and love with will be here. Just drive away from the clutter of the world, far from the noise and the busy world, then immerse yourself in the love you felt for all of your precious pets. Once you emerge from that, it's the first left. You'll know it when you see the tall trees and the colorful bridge."

I looked around. "Are your pets here?"

She shook her head. "My beloved pets are in my space. Everyone has their own special farm upstate, and someday they will all see their wonderful pets again. And now, you know this to be true."

I rubbed Shep's head, the big dog smiling from underneath his oversized jowls. As I looked around, the hawks became familiar. The field mice all looked like the ones that scurried through the barn all winter. The cats, the rabbits – I knew them all from some point in my past. I felt my affection for all these creatures return, flooding through me with a love overflowing my heart and washing across my body.

I've been a veterinarian for some time now, and I've traveled to the big farm upstate several times. I know the joy of those animals, the love they feel for us in life and how it carries on afterward. It is a feeling so powerful I sometimes cry.

Yesterday, I met with a family that had to put down their eighteen-year-old cat I had been treating for several years. There was no doubt in anyone's mind that the poor tabby was suffering, beyond help, and would not be alive for very long. The poor feline's life amounted to little more than one last compassionate act. Knowing what I know now, I could administer it without regret.

We all sat together during the injections, and I let the family know once their beloved tabby breathed her last. They wept just as any caring, loving family would, and I held their hands as long as they needed. When they finally looked at me, I felt what they experienced. They felt what I felt when I first met Dr. Chandra. They now knew peace. They understood this was not a bad day, just a transition. This was the sleep between today and tomorrow. They breathed deeply, forced a smile through the tears, and shook my hand in thanks.

There's always sorrow in losing a pet. But thanks to my mentor and friend, Dr. Chandra, I know it is not an end. That family will be with their tabby again. We all will. They never leave us and we never leave them. They just wait for that happy reunion at the big farm upstate.

Meet The Authors

Jane Binner (Jane.Binner@yahoo.com)

Jane Binner is a lifelong Illinois resident, currently in Kankakee where she is a part-time law student while working at a local law office. Writing is her first love, and Jane has won a few nominal awards. At this time, Jane facilitates a writers' workshop, while participating in others, and is currently working on a couple of non-fiction projects, along with a fiction piece which she is toying with the idea of turning into a graphic novel.

Norm Cowie (Norm.cowie@paramont-eo.com)

Norm Cowie is an award-winning business columnist and author of almost a dozen YA and adult books that reviewers compare to Douglas Adams' Hitchhiker's Guide to the Galaxy. He is a member of SCBWI, NSNC and several other organizations that identify themselves by a bunch of initials. He founded the Humor Writers of America because he likes to hang with people who think Whoopee Cushions are funny. Visit Norm at www.normcowie.com.

Awesome Angie Engstrom (angie@angieengstrom.com)

Humans make life too hard. Awesome Angie Engstrom brings simplicity to the complex issues of business and personal life. Her work as a Landscape Designer and Contractor, Professional Organizer, Elite Athlete and Fitness Professional, along with navigating extraordinary parenting challenges has led to a unique mastery of simplicity promoting well-being that has manifested into an incredibly entertaining and enlightening message that has impacted thousands of lives. Awesome Angie inspires everyone; her practical knowledge and profound personal insights exude contagious energy that inspires self-leadership and change. She is a rare blend of visionary, designer, and coach with the ability to speak to her truth, while touching the wisdom of our hearts. There is an unshakable mission in Awesome Angie's soul to instigate change, empower, and impact others to achieve more in less time so that they can live their life on purpose for greater productivity and play. Awesome Angie is the best-selling author of two books, *Overcoming Mediocrity* and *The One Thing Every Mom Needs To Know,* all found on Angie's website at www.AwesomeAngie.com. Through lessons learned from this story and many others, the Achieving More business seminars, workshops and coaching programs were developed. You can learn more at www.GettingYourselfUnstuck.com, including a free download to get you started. Follow her along on major social media channels at AwesomeAngieEngstrom. Awesome Angie lives in Downers Grove, Illinois with her husband, Mike, son, Michael, and schnauzer, Austin. She is known in her community as Awesome Angie because she honors the awesomeness in you.

Todd Hogan (rtoddhogan@gmail.com)

Todd Hogan is a voracious reader and writer whose short stories and poems have been published in ten regional anthologies. Two short plays have been chosen for performance in the Joliet Bicentennial Theater's Emerging Playwright Festival, the most recent performed on January 18, 2020. In the anthology, Stranded, available on Amazon, he included three short stories. In a forthcoming anthology, he has three short stories on the theme of hidden identity. He continues working on his novels.

Kathleen C. Z. Klevorn (kklevorn@comcast.net)

Kathy was born and grew up in southern Illinois. She attended St. Mary's Catholic School and Chester High School in Chester, Illinois. She earned a Bachelor's Degree in Medical Technology fron Quincy College in Quincy, Illinois. She has lived and worked in Missouri, New York, and Texas, Currently, she and her husband, Joe, live in New Lenox, Illinois. She enjoys reading, writing, cooking, exercise and visiting her three children who are now spread out across the country in Maryland, Idaho, and Illinois. Her first published stories are contained in this book.

Jeanne Meeks (clovemay48@yahoo.com)

Jeanne describes herself as an outdoors woman, a late bloomer, and a cheerleader for women who try. In 2007 she backpacked across the Grand Canyon where she was inspired by a tragedy to write her first novel. *Rim to Rim* was nominated at a 2014 Chicago writers convention for Best First Novel. Jeanne's Florida tennis teams supported her first two books, but teased her until she agreed to write a story around them. The Tennis Team Mysteries, *Gator Bait* and *Killer Serve*, were born. In 2018, *Killer Serve* made it to the semi-finals in the Illinois Soon To Be Famous Author Project. Jeanne comes from a family of ten, has two sons, loves wildflowers, tennis, kayaking, camping, reading, and long distance bicycling, and occasionally has fits of baking. She adores her five grandchildren and would love to teach them outdoor skills. After twenty-eight years in business, Ms. Meeks and her husband, Bob, sold their security surveillance company to a British corporation. Jeanne was a long-time Girl Scout leader, the President of the New Lenox Chamber of Commerce, and on the board of a local bank. Ms. Meeks now writes full-time and belongs to Mystery Writers of America.

Diane Perry (perry50rt@comcast.net)

Diane has a Bachelor of Arts in Journalism from Eastern Illinois University and worked as a newspaper reporter for the Star Suburban and Hammond Times. In her spare time, she enjoys companionship with her husband, Scott; dog, Ashlee and cat, Jynx. Diane and Scott enjoy travelling, bicycling, snow skiing, and play guitar together. She just recently published a book (2020) titled, *What Ruined Everything.* It can be purchased on Amazon.

Dawn E. Plestina (writerswe@use.startmail.com)

Dawn shares her writing with the desire to inspire people to reflect. Through that reflection, she hopes her readers take action to create a more positive world. The documentary, *Dying to Teach: The Killing of Mary Eve Thorson*, featured her reflective writing.

James Pressler (jpres96507@yahoo.com)

James is a career economist who uses creative writing as an outlet for his more playful side. He started writing for personal catharsis and growth, but it rapidly grew into a decades-long passion. His storytelling in the voices of children, ghosts and other characters brings new perspectives to familiar themes, with moods ranging from friendly humor to serious observations on the darker aspects of life. Having written short stories and character sketches for several years, James has also penned two novels.

Jolee L. Price (rjpcomp@aol.com)

Jolee feels that reading and writing intertwine, opening up the sphere of creativity of one's imagination. Fiction is her favorite theme, although she has written a few works of non-fiction and has had essays in both genres published. She attends the group because she wants to be a better writer, and the diversity of her fellow writers is amazing. They offer criticism in a most helpful, not condescending way, and provide tons of encouragement. The support offered is amazing and genuine. She feels that when one of the members has success with the publishing of a book, article or in just getting that first draft done, it is a group success.

Eric J. Stiltner (redraven84.es@gmail.com)

Eric is the younger of two sons and grew up in Romeoville, Illinois. Upon graduating from Romeoville High School in 2003, Eric received multiple awards and certificates in Culinary Arts and would later go on to college in that field. Even though he loved the art of cooking, he knew in his heart that his biggest passion has always been for writing. Eric has been on several mission trips throughout the world to places such as Mexico, Nicaragua and Haiti. He also is an animal lover and loves spending time with his family. Both sports and music have played a key role in his life. Eric was brought up in a Christian household and holds his faith very close to his heart. Anyone who knows him will say that he is a laid-back goofball!

Paula Morris Thomas (thomas17@ameritech.net)

A lifelong resident of the Lockport/Joliet, Illinois areas, Paula was bitten by the writing bug in the late 1980s when she discovered the joy of journaling. Her desire to be a published writer was heightened and honed beginning in November 2006 when she attended her first meeting at the New Lenox Library and met the founder of our literary family, Miles Snyder (deceased). Paula has enjoyed being included as one of the contributors of the three books that have been published by the New Lenox Writers' Group, and even created the cover art for the first book, *Writers, We*. In February 2017 she published her first solo book of 256 life points and words of encouragement titled *Life of Days*, available on Amazon. She is currently working on two more books that will be part of the *Life of Days* series.

Phyllis Tolen (ladydifarm@sbcglobal.net)

Phyllis was born in Marshall, Illinois while her father served overseas during WWII. She and her mother lived with her grandparents on a farm. She graduated from Marshall High School in 1961 and attended Eastern Illinois University where she met the love of her life, Don, who later became her husband. In 1964 she graduated with a degree in Elementary Education and started teaching at Oakland Grade School. There she taught 3rd and 4th grade where her classroom was started in the basement and then moved midyear to the gymnasium. In 1967-68, Phyllis and her husband joined the Peace Corps and moved to the Philippines. There she trained students to teach English and Math at the Leyte Normal School. Upon returning to the USA, she taught 4th-6th grade at Haven, Haines, and Bentley Schools in New Lenox. In 1984 she was honored as a Master Teacher of Will County and guided Bentley School to become recognized as a Blue Ribbon School. She and her husband, Don, retired in 1994. Teaching was the perfect profession for her, and upon retiring she often said, "Once my student, always my student."

Emilia Weindorfer (penguindor@comcast.net)

Emilia is a long-time member of the New Lenox Writers Group. She contributed six essays for the first anthology Writers We published by the group in 2014, and other essays for the subsequent anthologies. The group continues to inspire her with their multiple writing talents. She is retired after twenty-seven years of teaching and ten years as an elected trustee of the Mokena Library Board. She has four beautiful grandchildren. She and her husband Don have been married fifty-five years, and live in Mokena with their beloved rescue dog, Will.